25 tales
EVEN MORE APPALACHIAN GHOST STORIES & MYSTERIES

Also Availible from Howling Hills Publishing

---

23 Tales: Appalachian Ghost Stories, Legends & Mysteries
24 Tales: More Appalachian Ghost Stories, Legends & Mysteries
Open House: Mostly True Tales of Crazy in Southern Real Estate
East Tennessee Garden Stories

HOWLING HILLS PUBLISHING

Kingsport, Tennessee

HOWLING HILLS
Howling Hills is an independent publisher of quality nonfiction books. We're committed to telling stories from Greater Appalachia and focus on people, the outdoors, food, and the environment.
Learn more and connect with us at **howlinghillspublishing.com**.

EDITING
Terry Shaw

BOOK DESIGN
Alan O.W. Barnes
25 Tales: Even More Appalachian Ghost Stories & Mysteries
©2025 Howling Hills Publishing

First published in the United States of America in 2025 by Howling Hills Publishing, Kingsport, Tennessee.

Howling Hills Publishing, LLC
Kingsport, Tennessee
howlinghillspublishing.com.

All rights reserved. No part of this book may be reproduced in any form without written permission from the copyright owners.

All images in this book have been reproduced with the consent of the artists concerned, and every effort has been made to ensure accurate credits. We apologize if there are inaccuracies that may have occurred and will resolve inaccurate or missing information in subsequent reprintings of this book and/or at **howlinghillspublishing.com**.

ISBN: 979-8-9881621-4-8
CIP data is available through the Library of Congress.

CONTENTS

8	**INTRODUCTION** TERRY SHAW
11	**THE CAVE** TAYLOR FLOYD
18	**OUR GHOST IS A THIEF** PHYLLIS PRICE
24	**THE UNKIND RAVEN HAS MORE THAN BOOKS** LEAH GILKERSON & KAITLYN PARKER
28	**THE HOLLOW** JERRY SWORD
35	**GAINS GETS THE SKIP** MARK J. TIDWELL
40	**THE COMPANY HOUSE BED AND BREAKFAST** SUE WEAVER DUNLAP
45	**AN ENTITY, AN OUTSIDER** SUSAN TIDWELL BROWN
49	**A VISIT FROM THE MAYOR** SUZY TROTTA
54	**THRU THE NIGHT** ANNIKA RINGEN
60	**ELIZABETH** BRANDON WHITED
63	**THE BROKEN STONE OF SUNBRIGHT** PATTY IRELAND
73	**GHOSTLY VISIT** PATRICIA HOPE

CONTENTS

76	**ECHOES OF THE UNSEEN** RONDA CAUDILL
84	**THE NIGHT MARCHERS** ANNA WOOLIVER PHILLIPS
87	**DISMAL BLUFF** JOSHUA ANDERSON
92	**A MARK THAT STANDS THE TEST OF TIME** THOM TRACY
96	**SPIRITS OF OLD GRAY** LAURA STILL
102	**THE SHY MADAM** ALLISON CHURCHILL
106	**THE END OF THE LINE: BRUSHY MOUNTAIN** MATTHEW SORGE
112	**UNCLE LEON AND UNCLE ERNIE** SHARON LARISEY
114	**TIGER WOMAN** SHEREE COMBS
118	**THE HIGH RIDGE CHILD** EMILY MONROE
124	**THE ODD CASE OF THE REVEREND DOCTOR STEPHEN FOSTER** KEVIN SAYLOR
128	**MR. HARRISON'S HOUSE** CHRISSIE ANDERSON PETERS
133	**SHADOWS HAVE NO EYES** JAY HERRIN

YOU DON'T HAVE TO BELIEVE IN GHOSTS TO ENJOY A GOOD STORY

I don't believe in ghosts, but...

We hear that all the time, followed by whatever the teller experienced.

I get it.

Since Howling Hills started publishing ghost story anthologies in 2023, I've gotten it from readers, random strangers, even contributing writers. Ghost stories have been around since there have been people who could become ghosts. So has skepticism. For the record, I believe in ghosts. And I believe certain people are more attuned to what lingers on the other side—just as certain people have a better sense of smell or maybe eyesight. More than anything, I believe in the power of good stories, and I'm sure you can get behind that.

As in *23 Tales* and *24 Tales*, this volume is packed with family stories. **Taylor Floyd** starts off *25 Tales: Even More Appalachian Ghost Stories & Mysteries* with a gripping memory from her childhood set deep in the Great Smoky Mountains. **Jerry Sword** takes us back decades to his family farm in Russell County, Virginia. **Mark J. Tidwell** recalls an enduring tale of friendship between his father and another World War II veteran.

The stories are as varied as the writers. **Sue Weaver Dunlap** recounts an odd experience at her cousin's bed and breakfast. **Sharon Larisey** retells the tale she and her cousins heard about their great uncles during World War I. **Patricia Hope** tells of an encounter with a family legend in East Tennessee and **Sheree Combs** recalls shrieks of Tiger Woman from her childhood in Southeastern Kentucky.

Just east of where Sheree grew up, **Susan Tidwell Brown** had a chilling experience in her first year at Berea College. **Phyllis Price** knows a prankster ghost in another college town, Blacksburg, Virginia.

We have three stories set in workplaces: **Leah Gilkerson** and **Kaitlyn Parker** own a haunted bookstore, The Unkind Raven in Dandridge, Tennessee. **Brandon Whited** worked at a haunted hospital in Lebanon, Virginia. And **Allison Churchill** did time at a creepy newspaper in Keyser, West Virginia.

History and ghosts always go together. Paranormal investigator **Matthew Sorge** gives historical perspective to his chilling visits to the former Brushy Mountain State Penitentiary. In Northeast Pennsylvania, **Thom Tracy** explores a lingering legend of a hanging in the town of Jim Thorpe. **Joshua Anderson** explains how a spot in East Tennessee became known as Dismal Bluff. **Kevin Saylor** talks about events to bring back the dead in the early days of Knoxville. **Laura Still** explores the stories behind two graves at that city's Old Grey Cemetery. **Patty Ireland** and **Anna Wooliver Phillips** also weave history and cemeteries into their tales.

Then there are the haunted houses. **Ronda Caudill** grew up in a few and, as an adult, chooses to live in one. **Suzy Trotta** has lived in several but considers herself way scarier than any ghost. **Chrissie Anderson Peters** and **Emily Monroe** don't live in haunted houses but tell stories of friends who do. Or did.

Nature is woven throughout this anthology. **Annika Ringen** experienced it as much as anyone on a solo hike along Vermont's Long Tail. And the book concludes, as it begins, with a creepy story involving a cave, with **Jay Herrin** sharing a dark tale he heard set in Southwest Virginia.

Thanks to everyone who contributed!

Terry Shaw
Howling Hills Publishing

ONE
THE CAVE
COSBY, TENNESSEE

Taylor Floyd

As an only child in the remote Smokies, the trees were often my only friends. They spoke in creaks and rustles, and with the patience of the lonely, I learned to listen. I grew up in the hush between wind and whippoorwill, where silence wasn't empty... it was waiting. While my family worshiped in a one-room church, I found sanctuary beneath the forest canopy, in a cathedral of bark and shadow. But the woods held more than reverence. They held chill warnings, old folktales, and things that didn't stay where you left them.

Our holler curled like a question mark near Cosby, Tennessee, its secrets stitched between the ridgelines. My great-grandmother, Mamaw, lived at the head of it, where the rhododendrons grew thick and the air felt watchful. She was Irish by blood and by belief, and grew most of what we ate. On warm summer nights, when the corn whispered in the breeze, she'd tell me about thin places where the veil between this world and the next wore paper-thin, where time buckled, and the dead could still speak, if you knew how to listen.

I spent most days wandering through the woods, barefoot and singing, bounding between tree trunks like a fawn. The land back behind the house rose and fell in folds of damp moss and leaf mulch, shadowed by hickories and oaks. I knew those rolling hills like other children knew playgrounds or neighborhoods. I knew where the creek narrowed and deepened and where salamanders clung beneath flat stones. I knew which stumps would bleed amber sap and which hollows in the earth would sink beneath your step if you weren't careful. The woods were not a place I visited; they were part of me. My feet knew the paths the deer used, and my shadow stretched long among the forest floor when the sun began to tilt west.

Sometimes I would lie in the tall grass and close my eyes, letting the wind move through me as I imagined myself dissolving into roots, or rising into mist as something liminal, half-human. And sometimes, in that strange hush where birds fell silent and the air turned watchful, I felt the woods listening back. There was no fear in that. Only a reverence, an understanding deeper than language. I belonged to the land, and it, somehow, belonged to me. However, Mamaw had her worries. She didn't mind my wandering. She believed in the holiness of wild places. But she'd always pause a moment when I would head for the back door. Her eyes would fix on me like she was reading something only she could see, and she'd say it low, almost like a prayer:

"Be careful, darling," she murmured, rocking slowly on the porch. "Mind the dark places. Sun forgets 'em. But he don't.'

That was the first time I heard the tale of the Boogerman. Over the years, I've heard him called other things, a spook, a haint, but they all seem to fall under the same shadow. The Booger has no face, just a smooth stretch where eyes and mouth should be. He slithers between rocks, flat as a shadow, lurking in the cool, damp places where children wander when they shouldn't. His hearing is sharp as an owl's. A whisper, a snapped twig, even the hush of a frightened breath will draw him near. But he won't snatch you right away... oh no.

He waits.

He watches.

He lets the fear sink deep. Then the woods you had previously known twist strange, and you start to do foolish things. You forget the most basic rules, like don't leave the trail. That's when he reaches. Long fingers, cold as river stones that slip around you and drag you into the dark, where no one ever finds you again.

When you're young, you don't believe you could ever lose your way. I knew the woods, and the woods knew me. My feet always found the same path back out as the one that led me in. So I scoffed at her stories of people vanishing.

"There've been disappearances," she'd say from the porch, snapping a bean in half with a little pop. "People who stepped off the path and got turned around. Sometimes days go by, and they show up again... blank-eyed and starved, not a word in 'em. Other times..." She'd glance toward the woods, where the shadows gathered even in daylight. "Other times, the mountain keeps 'em."

"June of sixty-nine, Dennis Martin just vanished," she said. "One minute he was playin' with his cousins up by Spence Field, next minute he was gone. Park rangers, dogs, helicopters, all of 'em came out. Never found a bone."

I'd heard the story before, the version they told at school or around campfires when folks wanted to scare each other. But Mamaw's telling was different. There was no thrill in it, just something heavy and old, like iron in the blood

"They looked in the wrong places," she said, voice low. "They looked with maps and flashlights and logic. But the forest don't abide by any of that. I knew a man, volunteer firefighter, who was a part of the search party," she continued. "Said the woods went quiet that night. Not just still. Not natural. Even the bugs shut their mouths. Said they heard something, though, out past the treeline. A scream, but not a child's. Said it sounded like something trying to sound like a child."

I felt the hair on my arms stand up, but Mamaw kept going, steady as rain. "Some say he got took by a bear or fell down a hole. But there are certain hills and hollers you just don't wander in. Story says Cherokee wouldn't hunt in those parts after sundown. Said there were things older than God's name living in the stone."

She looked at me, and her eyes weren't cloudy that day. They were sharp and green as the moss on the north side of the trees.

As you can imagine, as a child this truly frightened me but not enough to keep me from those woods. Especially in the daunting boredom of the summer when I didn't have school to occupy my imagination. One day in particular I was restless enough to get my feet moving and decided to conquer a new mountain. I don't know what led me there, curiosity, perhaps, or some old hunger for discovery.

That was when I saw the cave. The entrance was set in the stone, half-hidden by vine and shadow. It looked less like a cave than a wound in the earth, the kind that never heals. I hesitated. Mamaw's voice prickled at the edge of memory. *There are places in this world that do not want to be found.*

But I was a child, and children are faithful only to wonder.

I slipped inside.

The coolness hit me first, sharp and wet, like the breath of something long buried. The walls were slick with veins of groundwater. I walked in slow, careful steps, with small amounts of sunlight catching jagged edges. Pulpy moss wept like a sponge under my touch. No light reached down there, not even the pale wash that clings to the backs of eyelids. It was a blind man's world, a tomb beneath the tombs. I thought of Jonah, swallowed whole, forced to sit in the belly of his punishment and reckon with his disobedience. I thought of hell, not the fire-and-brimstone hell Mamaw warned of, but the kind found in Psalms and Job: a Sheol, a pit, a silence so thick it snuffs out the soul.

That's when I heard the birdsong.

A single trill, too sweet for that darkness. It echoed strangely with a thin deliberateness. Whippoorwill, maybe. But wrong. The notes bent oddly, as if sung through a mouth unfamiliar with how sound is meant to work. Even as a child I knew something was wrong. What kind of bird sings in a place with no sky?

The song repeated, impossibly near. I could feel it in the rock around me, like it came from within the stone itself, not echoing, but emanating. My skin prickled, the way it does in church when the preacher says something that cuts a little too close. A verse rolled unbidden through my head, one Mamaw used to quote when she'd find a bird's nest tucked in the rafters of the porch: "Even the sparrow finds a home, and the swallow a nest for herself, where she may lay her young-near your altar, O Lord of hosts."

But this didn't feel like God's house. This was something older than altars, deeper than doctrine. There was no mercy in the air here, only waiting. And that wasn't His bird. It sang like it had heard the hymn once and twisted it into something lonesome and hollow. The way the Devil might hum a lullaby. Even then, I knew, not in my child's mind, but in my ancestors' marrow, that I was not meant to be there. That even if I walked back out into sunlight, I would not be leaving untouched. When I finally turned to run, the darkness clung to me like wet cloth. It took effort to remember the shape of the world. My hands trembled. My legs moved like they belonged to someone else. When I stumbled into the open, the light struck me, not gently, but like a slap. As if the sun had forgotten me and was startled to see me return. When I'd entered the cave, the sun had been high and hot above the trees. Now it filtered through the canopy in long, slanting rays, soft and golden. A hushed kind of light you only see in the last breath of day. I had only been in the cave a few minutes. Ten, at most. But the sun now sat at an angle that spoke of hours lost.

I ran all the way home with a weight in my chest. Not fear, exactly, but reverence. It felt as though I had brushed against something I wasn't meant to touch. Something that didn't speak in words, but in stillness, shadow, and sound. Mamaw was sitting on the porch, waiting, like she knew. She didn't scold me for coming home after dark. She didn't need to. She just looked at me, long and quiet, and I understood that she saw it, whatever it was, in my eyes. She knew I'd come close to something you can only meet alone.

The cave was gone after that. I tried to find it. I frequently retraced my steps, but I never saw it again. Still, sometimes when I hear a certain bird-song I stop. I listen. Not out of fear. Out of respect.

As an adult, I tell myself I must've dreamed it. That the mind of a child is soft clay. Easy to shape, easy to scare. I've read enough since then to understand how stories root in us, how folklore spreads like mold—quiet and persistent. Maybe that's all it was. And still, there is the birdsong. That single note, sudden and unexpected, threading the air like a promise. Even now, grown and far from that holler, I hear it. That birdsong. That *not-bird* birdsong. Soft, nearly sweet, rising from beneath the world like it never forgot me. Maybe, just maybe, the bird is still singing. Waiting for me to remember the way back.

TAYLOR FLOYD *grew up in the shadow of the Great Smoky Mountains, where evenings were often spent listening to folktales passed down by her Irish-descended family. Those early stories sparked a lifelong fascination with myth, mystery, and the hidden corners of the human heart. She went on to study literature and creative writing at the University of Tennessee, earning her bachelor's of arts degree. Her work often weaves folklore with lyrical* *prose and psychological depth, exploring the blurred lines between memory, myth, and reality.*

TWO
Our Ghost Is a Thief
Blacksburg, Virginia

Phyllis Price

Doug Songer served with pride as our local postmaster in the 1990s in Blacksburg, Virginia. He liked to look professional on the job, but when he married my niece Cathy, he chose jeans and a checkered shirt for the occasion. I missed the wedding, but years later would come to live on their small farm. The ceremony was held outdoors near his homeplace along Craig Creek. The location reflected their love of nature and an unpretentious lifestyle.

Nothing felt better to Doug than coming home at the end of the day and changing into comfortable clothes. But he preferred wearing suits and ties instead of casual dress clothing or postal employee uniforms when on the job. When you're the boss, it doesn't hurt to look the part.

One morning before work, Doug yelled from the shower for Cathy to lay out his blue pin-stripe suit and a good-looking tie to go with it. She checked the spot in the closet where it usually hung, but it was not there. Muttering to herself, she rummaged through hanging clothes, scanned the closet floor, and even checked *her* closet. "I don't see it, Honey," she called out, perplexed.

"Look again," he replied. "It's got to be there, unless you took it to the cleaners." She checked again, but it was nowhere to be found.

How can a man's suit go missing!?

Showered and shaved, Doug chose another outfit for the day—khakis and a dark blue blazer. Not bad, he thought, but where's my suit? "Maybe Uncle Arch took it," he quipped with a wink and a laugh, adjusting his tie on the way out the door.

"Oh, no, not Uncle Arch," Cathy groaned aloud in the quiet house after he left.

Determined to solve the latest conundrum, she did a thorough sweep of areas she previously checked. The search was futile.

Perplexed to the point of frustration, she decided to drive to the dry cleaners on the off chance it was there. Stepping up to the counter, she asked to speak to the manager whom she knew well. "I know you think I'm crazy, but Doug's suit is missing. I wonder if I dropped it off and forgot about it," she said, laughing aloud. She described the suit in detail, hoping to jog the manager's memory.

After combing both the work room and the carousel where clothing hung waiting for pickup, the manager returned to the front counter. "Cathy, I'm sorry. His suit is just not here. And I don't recall your dropping off cleaning anytime recently. But give me a call if I can be of any further help."

Disappointed, and more perplexed than ever, she left without it.

That evening over dinner, Cathy relayed the story of the visit to the cleaners. "Maybe you changed clothes at Johnny's house after church before a cookout or something," she offered, desperate for an explanation. "Could we have taken it on a trip and left it somewhere?"

But in his free time, Doug was a casual dresser.

"There's no way I'd have taken one of my suits on a trip unless we were going to a wedding or a funeral," he replied.

He's right, she thought.

The plot thickened.

Eventually, the suit search ended. The mystery was mentioned only in passing with a roll of the eyes or a soft chuckle. Weeks passed. Then one morning Cathy opened the closet door to find all the hanging clothes pushed to either side on the rod and the missing suit hanging by itself, directly in front of her.

"Doug! Doug!" Cathy screamed. "He's at it again! Uncle Arch had your suit!"

David Songer, Doug's brother, has his own stories about Uncle Arch's shenanigans. One goes like this:

As a working man, David had only weekends to do laundry, housekeeping, and yard work. His Sunday morning routine was to grab a newspaper and head to the laundromat where he caught up on local news while the washer gurgled and sloshed, the dryer heated and spun his clothes clean. It was a relaxing, almost comforting, way for a young, single man to spend a Sabbath morning. But not this Sunday.

David fed his dog, gathered his dirty clothes, and left home early, stopping to buy gas and a newspaper on the way. He arrived in time to avoid the rush on washers and dryers. He found several machines empty when he walked into the warm, sweet-smelling Mr. Suds. "Hey, how's it going?" he called to the attendant. "Looks like I'm in luck!"

"I reckon you are. Nobody shows up this early," replied the middle-aged, blond-haired woman who kept the place swept, lint filters cleaned, and loiterers off the premises.

Reaching into a hip pocket for his wallet, David found it empty. He patted all his pockets where the wallet might be. Nothing! A thoughtful man who liked to plan, he couldn't believe he had lost it. The day before he even made sure he had correct change for the machines.

"My wallet's gone!" he yelled to the attendant. "I just bought gas and a paper. Must have left it at the station. I'll be back."

He rushed to his car. Before driving off, he searched car seats, floorboards, glove box, and dashboard. Filled with the heart-sick panic one feels when a wallet goes missing, he pushed the speed limit on the way back to the gas station.

Like the laundromat, the gas station had few customers at that early hour. "Nobody's been here since you left," the clerk responded when David asked about the wallet. "You're welcome to look around." A search of the area near the newspaper rack and the parking lot where he had pumped gas revealed nothing.

He hurried home, but knew the wallet couldn't be there because of the earlier purchases. His habit was to leave it in the car, but he felt obligated to check the house just to be sure it wasn't there. He quickly scoured drawers, tabletops, shelves, closets, clothing pockets, bedding, underneath furniture, even kitchen cabinets. Nothing.

Deeper panic set in. Not only had he lost precious money, but a credit card, driver's license, insurance card, and personal identification were compromised. Losing cash was one thing, but the prospect of having a culprit running up charges on a credit card was horrifying!

In a pre-digital age, David slogged his way through the process of ordering a new license and replacing other credentials. But it was the loss of the credit card that worried him most. He was forced to wait a month for the paper statement to arrive. On the day it appeared in his mailbox, he ripped it from the envelope. He couldn't believe his eyes. No suspicious charges! At least that was something. He breathed a sigh of relief.

The following morning David awoke from the first good night of sleep since the wallet went missing. Anticipating that first sip of coffee to start the day, he jumped out of bed and headed for the kitchen. After filling the coffee pot with cold, crisp well water, he scooped the aromatic grounds into the basket and pressed the switch. Opening the cabinet door, he reached for the cup he used every day. There, on top of the mug, lay his wallet—supple leather, worn in the familiar pattern, edges curved from age and use. *Blast that Uncle Arch!!*

Over the years we all heard stories about David's and Doug's late Uncle Arch—a jovial, easy-going man who loved to joke, tease, and pull pranks on people. Not much changed in the afterlife. He lived adjacent to the old homeplace where he was raised, and where members of the Songer clan still live. His thievery appears to be restricted to the small group of people who inhabit his familiar turf.

At first, the phenomenon was regarded as coincidence. Relatives' belongings began to disappear—tools, eyeglasses, credit cards, books—everyday items of pleasure and necessity. But as time went on, victims shared stories and recognized a pattern. An item disappeared, owners became frantic with worry, doubted themselves, or blamed others for the loss. Searches were extensive and obsessive. Hair pulled out, swear words sometimes uttered. Eventually, efforts to recover items stopped, emotions cooled, the lost was found—or replaced—and the incident was forgotten.

Arch is buried down the hill in the family cemetery. But I'm not scared. He is not the sort of spirit to slip the bonds of his grave at night, creep across squeaky floors, or appear as an apparition dressed in black, as witnessed by his sister shortly before her death.

I stop by his gravesite sometimes in passing, tap his stone with my walking stick. "Hey, you, we know what you're up to, and it's not funny!"

He is unimpressed.

I am open to mystery. I accept that the veil between planes of existence is as thin as breath. But I find the idea of a man's suit or a wallet vanishing, then reappearing, blatantly outrageous. Still, I admit I am waiting for my favorite letter opener to show up any day now.

PHYLLIS PRICE *writes from a small farm in Southwest Virginia. Her work appears, or is upcoming, in* Artemis, Pine Mountain Sand & Gravel, Steamship Review, Main Street Rag, POEM, Anthology of Appalachian Writers, *and other journals, including the chapbook* Quarry Song. *Her work focuses on our interconnectedness with the natural world.*

THREE
THE UNKIND RAVEN HAS MORE THAN BOOKS

DANDRIDGE, TENNESSEE

Leah Gilkerson
&
Kaitlyn Parker

In every used bookstore, there's a certain quiet magic—the soft scent of worn pages mingling with dust, the gentle creak of wooden shelves that invite you to lose yourself among stories waiting to be discovered. The people inside are friendly, always ready to share a recommendation or a smile. At The Unkind Raven, you'll find that same warmth and welcome, but here, there's something quietly different just below the surface. Alongside the comforting whisp of pages turning, the walls seem to hold whispers of the past, and the floorboards softly echo with memories that linger just beyond sight. It's a subtle feeling, like a breath caught in the room or a shadow just beyond your vision—an unspoken presence that watches quietly, neither threatening nor gone.

Almost daily, we hear footsteps overhead in empty rooms, the rustle of unseen papers, or the soft thud of items falling from untouched shelves. Fleeting shadows move just out of view, and strange whispers sometimes ride the wind. But the house doesn't carry malice. Instead, it feels protective. Welcoming. As if the spirits inside have chosen to watch over it, rather than haunt it. From the moment we stepped inside to explore the space for our bookstore, we felt it: a quiet sense of comfort, like the home was glad to see us. That feeling stayed with us as we began to transform it into The Unkind Raven.

Naturally, our curiosity led us to research the home's history. We were delighted to learn the family of the late Judge Robert Hynds had once called it home. They were respected members of the community with deep roots in law, education, and literature. The house at 1214 Gay Street has hosted several esteemed tenants over the years—lawyers, teachers, and authors, including beloved newspaper columnist Bert Vincent. During the Civil War, the home served as headquarters for both the Union and the Confederacy (though not at the same time), and later, a field hospital.

With such a storied past, it's no surprise the house might hold onto a few echoes of its previous occupants. But nothing prepared us for that cold February evening—not stormy, but bitter enough to sink into your bones. We'd been running The Unkind Raven for just a short time and were getting used to the rhythms of the old house.

One night, we accidentally left a recorder running. When we listened the next morning, we froze. There were voices— soft, blurred, impossible to understand. Pages shuffled in the background, though no one had been in the shop. We exchanged wary glances but brushed it off until curiosity won. We left the recorder running again.

That evening, Kaitlyn stayed late to close. The sky darkened early, and by the time she locked up, it was just her and the chill. While on the phone, Leah's voice was in Kaitlyn's ear via earbuds as she moved through her closing routine. They had just installed security cameras and were still positioning them. Kaitlyn laughed nervously and said aloud, "If anyone would like to communicate or let us know you're here, you can walk in front of the cameras or speak into the black box on the stairs."

A joke. Mostly.

Then, Kaitlyn turned off the lights. The store grew silent, save for the creak of old floorboards settling in the cold. Leah monitored the cameras as Kaitlyn stepped outside. That's when she saw him. A man stood by the window near the front door. He looked clean and pressed, like someone stepping out of a different era: a fedora, button-down shirt, jacket, pleated pants, and loafers. It was as if he had walked straight out of another time.

He spoke first. "Hello, I didn't mean to startle you."

Kaitlyn jumped. "Oh! That's okay. I get jumpy at night. We're closed now, but we reopen at nine in the morning."

Leah's voice buzzed in her ear. "Who are you talking to?"

The man glanced at the building. "What is this place?"

"It's a bookstore," Kaitlyn said. "Leah and I own it."

He smiled, slightly crooked. "Oh wow. Good for you."

Leah again: "I still don't see anyone. Who are you talking to?"

"Thank you!" Kaitlyn said, smiling politely. "Come visit us tomorrow!"

"Okay," he replied, stepping back. "Have a good night." Then he turned and walked off the porch.

Then Kaitlyn said into the phone, "Leah, I was talking to the man standing by the window."

There was a pause. "There was no one there," Leah said. "I was looking at the camera the whole time."

Kaitlyn stepped into the street. Her car was the only one parked. The sidewalk was empty.

No movement. No sound. No man.

That moment stays with us.

Our little town of Dandridge is renowned for its rich history of ghost stories and unexplained sightings. Local police, longtime residents, and shop owners all agree: This is a tightly knit community shared by both the living and those gone before us. Among the many storied buildings here, the Hynds House is no exception.

It was during our research into the house's past that we discovered a photo of Bert Vincent, a beloved writer for the *Knoxville News-Sentinel*. He had lived and worked in this very building, his presence still felt by some. Was it him Kaitlyn spoke to that night? A curious spirit checking in on the new tenants? We'll never know for sure. But every now and then, when the shop is quiet and the shadows move just right, we wonder if he's still nearby—watching, writing, or simply waiting to be remembered.

LEAH GILKERSON *and* **KAITLYN PARKER** *co-own The Unkind Raven in Dandridge, Tennessee. Leah, originally from California and Hawaii, is a devoted wife and mother of three who finds joy in books, travel, and the quiet rhythm of country life. Kaitlyn, born and raised in Jefferson County, Tennessee, is a creative spirit who spent time living in Guatemala and now shares life in Dandridge with her boyfriend and their two beloved dogs. Best friends and next-door neighbors, Leah and Kaitlyn share a love of storytelling, quiet mornings, and finding beauty in the everyday.*

— FOUR —
THE HOLLOW
RUSSELL COUNTY, VIRGINIA

Jerry Sword

The Devil always shows up when you least expect him. That's what they say, and I've come to believe it. Not because I saw him—but because my brother did.

In 1978, I was only four years old, waiting in Florida with Mom and my sister, still too young to know what secrets the world could hide. My older brother Robert had travelled to the mountains of Virginia with our father. They had gone up to check on the family farm near Elk Garden in Corn Valley, places that don't show up on maps unless you already know where to look.

The power was turned off at the farmhouse since no one was living there. So they stayed with Willie, our half-brother, and his wife Opal. Willie was Dad's son from his first marriage, but by the time I came around, he felt more like an uncle–or something older still. The age gap was wide enough to make categories useless, and it was confusing to those outside our family. I remember the kids at school didn't understand how our brother was so much older; at times I found the age differences to be embarrassing. Now the only embarrassment I feel is that I ever cared what others thought. Family was family, and Willie was my brother. My peers have come and gone.

His house sat low, a working man's place he built on land Dad gave him, three bedrooms and a basement that felt like it knew things. There was no television—Opal wouldn't hear of it. She seemed to believe it opened the door to Satan himself, and I'm still not certain she was wrong about that. She wore her skirts down to her ankles. Jeans and makeup were forbidden, and so was sin. Crosses and other religious pieces hung on every wall, a constant reminder that God was watching. Prayer books with worn pages sat by the lamp though Robert didn't pay them much mind. Willie was a quiet man. Like a cowboy stepping out of a Western, he looked you in the eyes, with a voice as soft as a low wind. He'd nod, or offer you a seat, but he never pushed. Dad respected that about his son, and my father's respect had to be earned. My dad was a good man, but he was also a stern man.

Robert and Dad worked the farm by day for a couple of weeks. Dad fixed fences, his hands steadily twisting wire, like he owned the mountains, which he did. He was seventy-one, but you would never know it—he was tough, because he had to be, and it never faded. His own father had passed on when he was only sixteen, making him the man of the house. He finished raising his siblings and would marry and have five children, one of them being Willie.

My father had lived a full lifetime before he met Mom, and then he started over and did it again, raising seven children with her. Robert, who wanted desperately to be a man at fifteen, hauled posts and did my father's bidding for the entire two weeks. Sweat stung his eyes as he tried to keep up, wanting Dad's nod, the kind that said you were enough. That's how it was with him. I wasn't there, but I grew to know those days as well—work till you drop, then home to the family. At the end of that two weeks, Robert had gotten the nod he needed.

The night before they were to leave Virginia to travel back home, Opal prepared a feast that had been grown right there on my family's land. Summer nights at Willie's house were warm and lived in, making even a stranger feel at home. They would all sit—Willie, Opal, their daughter Debbie, Dad, and Robert—around a table heavy with life. Willie would ask Dad about the land or the cattle, and Dad's answers were short and to the point, his voice holding the attention of the room. Nobody ever tried to speak over him.

Dinner had been served and devoured. Opal brought out her blueberry pies, sweet enough to pull you in for more, while Willie listened as Debbie talked about her friends. The fallen dusk outside the house was filled with fireflies, but then something felt different. The air turned cold and heavy, like something settled in the room. It was the kind of cold that makes you check the door, even in summer. Robert felt the shift, but Dad's look said get to bed, so they went.

Willie and Opal headed to their bedroom, Debbie to hers, Dad to the third. Robert took the living room sofa, lumpy and rough against his back. Two of the bedroom doors stood close—Dad's open a little, Willie's shut tight—with darkness between them. Willie's bluetick hound let out a howl outside in the distance, lonesome and reverberating through the valley. Then it stopped, and the house went quiet, like it was waiting for something to happen.

Robert lay there for a long while, staring at the ceiling. The crosses on the walls were Opal's way of showing reverence for her Lord and Savior and could still be seen even though the lights were off, courtesy of the cool moonlight diffusing through the curtains. The mountains outside felt closer and seemed to be pressing in. Then he sensed it—a presence within the silence: no noise, just a weight in the air. Robert's heart started pounding, and he blinked, catching a shape in the doorway, or maybe the hall. It wore a white gown, tattered and frayed, like it had been left to rot. Long, dark hair fell loose, wild, and wrong. He thought for a moment that Debbie was pulling a prank.

"Debbie, is that you?" he called, his voice cracking.

No answer came.

"What do you want?" he tried again, only to be met with silence.

It didn't walk, but glided toward him, gown trailing slow, like a shadow you can't trust.

His gut twisted, but he stayed put, trying to be tough like Dad or at least act it.

It wasn't Debbie. It moved right to the sofa and leaned down, so close Robert couldn't breathe. Its face was black and hollow, with a gaping mouth, a faint skull flickering underneath, and no eyes, just a void that pulled at him.

The silence hit Robert like a wall—no hound, no creak, no air in his lungs. His jaw locked tight, and he couldn't scream, though his head was shouting that this couldn't be real. His arms wouldn't move, his eyes burned like fire. It stayed there, inches away, hollow, taking something from him, and leaving him with a memory that would terrify him for the rest of his life. He fought it internally, with the darkness pressing down hard. Then it turned, glided into Dad's room, and was gone. Robert blacked out cold, the sofa the only thing keeping him from falling apart.

Morning came, bright with sunlight cutting through the windows. When Robert woke he was soaked. The air around him was heavy like it held onto the night. Breakfast didn't help. He sat there, saying nothing, fork still in his hand. Willie sipped his coffee, not noticing anything off or out of sorts. Opal had served up breakfast, the same as every other morning. Debbie ate, her long, dark hair making Robert look twice. He stared at her. He couldn't stop, and then he heard it—a murmur, like voices tangled in a storm, too faint to grasp. Were they whispering? Hissing? Something bitter in them swelled, then broke, leaving him shaken, though nobody else looked up. Dad sat steady, like he carried everything. Robert's chest ached—the sounds in his head clawing at him, gone as quickly as they came.

Debbie looked up and asked, "Are you OK?"

His hands were shaking, and the food tasted bitter. The hound was howling outside, low, like it carried the night with it.

"Was that you last night?" Robert asked quietly.

Debbie's eyes went dark, no trace of a smile. She clearly had no idea what he was talking about. "Wasn't me," she said, voice tight, like she now felt something off, too.

Opal stayed quiet and began to clean up the kitchen while Willie kept his easy way, having no clue what had occurred just hours before. Robert couldn't say another word. Dad was sitting calmly across the table, seeing through him like he always did.

They left for home that morning, heading back to Florida. The hound's howl followed them, thin but sharp, like it knew more than it should. It followed them across the field between Willie's house and the old farmhouse we would move back to two years later. Once there was significant distance between them and Willie's house Dad spoke, steady, no shake in his voice.

"It's OK, I saw it too." He'd seen it from his bed—the tattered gown, the dark flowing hair—and he knew things like that happened. He saw no need to make a fuss about it. Robert nodded, didn't speak, his chest heavy like a rock. That night stayed with him, and it may be why he left at seventeen, seeking something tougher than fear—a story for another time. I wasn't there, but when Robert told me, years later, I felt it—the hollow of that night, the way it didn't let go. That face wasn't welcome, and it didn't care.

In 1980, my family moved back to Dad's old farmhouse. The fences were fixed, and the power was on again. As I got older, I would walk those fields at dusk, fireflies lighting the way, and from that young age I could feel it—the hollow. The presence there was not just something Robert imagined but something ancient, tied to the land, to the mountains, and to the fabric of time itself.

I left home thirty-three years ago, and I know nothing has changed there since. It's just older, and the vegetation is more dense and unforgiving. I still drive there every now and again to remember. And to forget. Sometimes I lie awake at night and thoughts of that place and time weigh heavily. A longing to go back coupled with the desire to never see it again.

The Devil always shows up when you least expect him. That's what they say, and I've come to believe it. On a winter's day in 2008, I walked to my mailbox. I opened it to be surprised by a large yellow envelope. The bubble-wrapped package was from L. B. Taylor Jr., an author from Williamsburg. We had developed a friendship as a result of my reaching out to tell him about unexplainable events in my life.

Although I never met him in person, we talked periodically, and I spent many hours telling him about things most people would find unbelievable. But not L.B. He was the author of over fifty books, including the *Ghosts of Virginia* series. I opened the envelope to find a copy of his latest book, *The Ghosts of Virginia Volume XIII*. I thumbed through the book while still at my mailbox, then stopped as I caught sight of the illustration marking the beginning of a chapter. The illustration perfectly fit the description of what my brother saw back in 1978. The story itself was about a banshee. Though I had heard the term, I was unfamiliar with the actual meaning. Still standing in my driveway, I dug my phone from my pocket, snapped a picture of the illustration, and sent it to my brother's phone. There was no message attached. Only the photograph. In a matter of seconds, my phone was ringing, with Robert on the other end.

"Where did you get that?" His voice was deadly serious.

I explained what it was and how it came into my possession. Then I asked, "Does it look familiar?"

"Yes, little brother, that's what I saw…"

A pause hung heavy, his breath uneven, like that night in 1978 was clawing back. Robert, always unafraid and quick to shrug off trouble, sounded small, the banshee's void still gripping him. "Gotta go, little brother," he said, voice tight, and the line went dead.

I stood there, Taylor's book in hand, feeling the weight of his fear, the same I'd felt when he first told me of the event decades ago. My talks with Taylor about shadows and things most wouldn't believe made this real. That illustration wasn't just ink; it was proof something ancient had touched our family. I carry that hollowness now, the shadow of that night, and sometimes I wake up in the still hours before dawn, knowing the Devil is never far away.

JERRY SWORD *is a storyteller who grew up in Russell County, Virginia and now lives in Bristol. He composed the song* Dead Man's Hands *for the American World Pictures movie "Grizzly Park." He has also written and directed the documentaries* This Place is Haunted *(2013) and* Season of the Witch *(2022). He's at work on the documentary* Under Broken Sky. *His story* A Haunting in Corn Valley *appeared in* 24 Tales: More Appalachian Ghost Stories, Legends & Mysteries.

FIVE

Gains Gets the Skip

JELLICO, TENNESSEE

Mark J. Tidwell

My father and his friend Gains had a tight, enduring friendship. Both grew up poor in the shadows of the Pine Mountain Range that marched toward Middlesboro, Kentucky from Campbell County, Tennessee. Both were members of the Greatest Generation. Both were avid ham radio enthusiasts. They were also private, quiet, hardworking men.

Dad worked the night shift bulldozing to grade specifications on Interstate 75 construction. Arriving home dust covered at six in the morning, he stripped his coveralls and washed up to carry the mail on the hilly streets of Jellico, Tennessee. He evaded biting dogs and hefted the mail pack all over town. Determined to snag a full-time US Postal Service job, he gutted it out for two years and provided a better life for his family, later being promoted to assistant postmaster. Gains, likewise, worked hard in manufacturing up north to make a living. Later, he came back home and worked and farmed.

Gains was a familiar figure leaning on our weathered rail fence, his old Chevy truck parked by the road. He and Dad talked ham radio on the cool front porch, around the wood kitchen table, or in Dad's smoke-filled radio room. At times, the tobacco smell was so strong you could taste it. Even now, the faint smell of his Lucky

Strikes emanates from the paneled walls. It is a hallowed space in the home where my wife Yvonne and I now live.

These guys were serious ham radio operators. They routinely talked all around the world via amateur radio. Our family often heard Daddy talk about the *skip* being in, a phenomenon that allowed radio contact with otherwise impossible locations. Dad explained this as radio waves bouncing off the ionosphere. From the skip being in, he had netted a tall, colorful stack of ham radio confirmation cards. I was raised looking at atlases of the globe with x's denoting all the countries he had communicated with. He had attained membership in the DX Century Club, a high honor among ham radio operators of verified communications with 100 countries. Before he passed away, Dad pushed that total to more than 280 countries and territories.

One sunny afternoon as Dad swung in his old porch swing, and Gains rocked in a white, slatted rocking chair, World War II came up in conversation. Since virtually every able-bodied man of their generation had served a hitch at the behest of Uncle Sam, neither considered their service in the United States Navy out of the ordinary.

What they didn't have in common was that Dad's ship, the destroyer USS Lyman K. Swenson, returned home safely. Gains's ship, the USS Houston, was sunk from a Japanese torpedo attack in the Java Sea on February 28, 1942. Only 368 out of 1,060 sailors survived. Perhaps these were not the lucky ones, as surviving soon led to capture by the Japanese and internment as prisoners of war in Thailand.

That afternoon, in great detail, Gains told of his ordeal.

The horrendous conditions included forced marches, starvation, torture, and slave labor on the "Death Railway." Gains helped build a bridge over the River Kwai. This continued for three and a half years and the number of Houston sailors steadily dwindled until only 291 were alive at the end of WWII.

"I didn't think I would live through it, or ever get home," Gains concluded.

The two friends spoke every day. If Gains was not talking to Dad over the fence rails or on the porch, he would often call. Phones were tethered devices then, hanging on walls. I often answered to hear Gains excitedly ask for Dad so he could tell him about some event happening on the ham radio scene. On May 15, 1978, Dad picked up the phone to an extra-excited Gains. Something huge was happening on the radio waves, akin to the gold truck coming through Mayberry on an Andy Griffith episode. Before he could tell dad the specifics, he exclaimed, "Jim, my barn is on fire! I'll call you back."

Those were the last words Gains ever spoke to Dad on earth. Within minutes, after running 100 yards uphill to battle the fire, he died from a massive heart attack. After all he had been through, Gains died at age 57, fighting the flames rumored to be ignited by some teenagers smoking dope in his old, gray barn. My dad, a tough man who generally showed little emotion, was visibly crushed by the loss of his good friend Gains Willard Lawson.

A few days after attending Gains's funeral and burial, my mother and I heard high frequency sounds from the radio room. Dad was at the Jellico Post Office on duty. We were quite used to all the radio sounds from his Swan equipment. However, the dit-dit-dot of his Morse code key was sounding off. It was plain as day, chattering through the house, though the transponder was not connected to any power source. Even stranger, it was in a desk drawer with the cord coiled around the base. Mother removed the cord, leaving it unconnected, and placed the transponder on his desk.

When Dad came home that evening, Mother and I described what we had heard and seen. Dad explained it away by saying, "Well, we live near the railroad. A train shook it and caused it to go off. There's the rock quarry, they blast and drill and work. That may have set it off."

We thought little more of the matter, until it happened again, and again, occurrences Dad dismissed. He was in denial, especially when we once more pointed out the tapper had no juice.

Then one day it happened at exactly the right time—Dad was home for lunch. The rock quarry crew was also on lunch break with nary an equipment sound arising from the place. No L&N freight train was blowing at the Highcliff crossing. Just as Dad was about to stuff a forkful of fried apple pie in his mouth, the sound came through the dining room clearly. Morse code blared out. I saw his expression transform to a troubled look, so rarely seen on his face. Mother and I did not read Morse code and had no idea what he was interpreting as the dits and dots sounded out.

Before Dad could gather his thoughts and say anything, my mother reached a hand over and touched his arm gently. "Junior, that is Gains trying to tell you something. You go in there and answer him back. This can't go on any longer."

Dad agreed and got up from the dinner table. He moved like he had been gut-punched. As we watched from the dining room, he proceeded into the radio room and pulled the Morse code key close. With head bowed, slowly at first, then picking up tempo, he tapped out a message.

Mother and I had stopped eating, for dinner was surely over.

Dad was visibly moved when he came back. It was not the time to ask questions. The hurt was too fresh. I never asked what he tapped out to Gains that day. I don't think my mother did, either. It was something we never discussed again.

My sister Susan and I believe the messages were a ham radio

73, goodbye ole buddy, good luck crossing over; and *77, long live our Morse code.* Messages obviously came through and were answered. All I can tell you is that the Morse code key never, ever again uttered another unexpected dit, dash or dot, as long as Dad lived and radioed.

James W. Tidwell Jr. passed away in 1999 after a hard-fought battle with ALS, twenty-one years after that last phone call and follow-on Morse code conversation from the other side. I'm quite certain the two old Navy salts and country boys from the rough mountains had a lot of catching up to do.

My mother Wilma, brother Ray, and sister Susan agreed that God would not deny Gains, who had suffered hell on earth, his last wish to say goodbye to his friend before he traveled to heaven. Susan firmly believes God energized a divine skip at just the precise angle to connect two friends a final time.

A lifelong resident of Highcliff, Tennessee, **MARK J. TIDWELL** *holds a bachelor's degree from Cumberland College and is a certified public library manager. He's been director of the Jellico Public Library for twenty-one years and has written more than 1,000 columns for The LaFollette Press. Tidwell is active in promoting local history, veterans' causes, and storytelling. He and his wife, Yvonne, enjoy tending plants in greenhouses and gardens, and spending time with their people and dog families. He is not a particular believer in ghosts but knows there is always the unexpected—and unexplained.*

SIX

THE COMPANY HOUSE BED AND BREAKFAST

DUCKTOWN, TENNESSEE

Sue Weaver Dunlap

Mama's been gone thirty-one years come July. I'm told whenever I meet up with folks who knew her back then, neighbors and kin, that I look more and more like her every day, especially now that I'm letting my hair go gray. Whenever I hear such, my heart swells with something akin to pride. My mama was a beautiful woman on up to the day she passed away. And all five foot two inches of Sarah Elizabeth Goode Weaver was a force to reckon with, living or dead.

Lizzie, as most folks called her, wasn't much of a talker. Kept most things to herself unless a body crossed the line and made her mad or if she was sharing family stories. I tried my best not to make her mad, especially when I was switching age. What secrets I didn't find out about by eavesdropping on family conversations Mama gladly shared with me, especially anything to do with ghosts or visitations or feelings.

When I shared my first experience with the sight, Mama and Daddy were startled. Daddy told her to do something about me while Mama cautioned me not to talk about it. As I grew older, Mama became more adamant that I learn to tamp down any special feelings or visions I had; didn't want me to appear any stranger that I already was to most people.

Since most of our women folk had experiences with the sight, none of the cousins were startled the day Mama started talking about the ghosts in Old Doc Kimsey's house on Main Street in Ducktown, Tennessee. I had driven her down that day to see the house my cousin Margie was thinking about buying to convert into a bed and breakfast. We were all standing around in the yard giving this rundown 1850s house the once over. It had been everything from Doc Kimsey's clinic to a seedy apartment house. Most everyone gathered that day "naysaid" Margie undertaking such a tremendous task.

The more we stood around chatting among ourselves, the quieter Mama became. When pressed by Margie about what she thought, Mama said, "Perhaps you better think hard about stirring up this house, its dust and what not."

Margie said, "What do you mean by what not?"

"Well, this place was a clinic for a long time," Mama said. "Several of our own kin had surgeries in Doc Kimsey's office on the ground floor. Look close at this end of the front porch. See the outline of a door that has been boarded over. That's where patients came and went. The front room is where he doctored them or did surgery. Folks around here have talked for years about young and old dying in this place."

Everyone stood around and chewed on that for a bit. Mama was done with her say and couldn't be coaxed to tell anymore.

By summer of 1994, The Company House Bed and Breakfast was ready to open for business. However, before we could officially take in guests, all of the rooms had to be slept in for a trial run. Margie had named the six rooms after the mines in the Copper Basin area. This particular night I chose the Isabella Room to sleep in. I stayed up pretty late in the parlor, one lamp on nearby so I could read. Everyone else had retired for the evening.

Old houses creak and moan, the give and take wood acquires over time as though it's still alive. Expansion and contraction. I heard all the suspect noises—footsteps on the stairs, the Hiawassee Room shutter rattling, and the glass pane of the old clinic door vibrating with the faint echo of a service bell clinging. Nothing unnerved me as I continued to read, determined to finish my book before going to bed. Afterall, I had nothing to fear. All of the cousins, and even Mama herself, had withstood the violent rocking chair noises of Aunt Joyce's ghost in her house over near Mineral Bluff.

Eventually things quieted completely, and I finished my book in peace. Giving one last look around the room, I glanced up before standing. That's when I saw her, a young girl in her early twenties, her brown hair flowing down her back like a long cape. Slender built, she was dressed for bed. She gathered the fabric of her peignoir in her hand, lifting the hem before descending the staircase. At the landing she glanced to her right as though she were expecting someone and then to her left. I suppose she thought her path was clear, and she stepped across the hall to the Isabella Room on the first floor. Her slender hand rested on the doorknob as she turned to give me a good-night bid. Then she was gone, disappearing into my room for the night.

In a bit, I gathered my own things and went down the hall to the Isabella Room. My hand paused over the doorknob as though I was searching for my own "the coast is clear" alert. I grasped the warm doorknob, turned it, and entered. The room was quiet, resting in the glow from the sconced lights over the bed and a dim light from the bathroom. Perhaps she knew her way out or decided to rest somewhere else in the room. Whatever the case, she left a happy radiance there in the Isabella Room that night.

For years, I was loathe to discuss my late-night visitor, perhaps because I wanted her to be my secret. For years, she visited me every time I spent the night. She seemed to be drawn to the Isabella Room and the old clinic which had been converted into a library. Since it had its own door, I always suspected she roamed around from those vantage points. One morning at breakfast, I finally asked Margie if she had ever witnessed anything ethereal near the Isabella Room. Without pause, she said, "Of course. She wanders the downstairs most nights. But don't mention her to anyone, especially guests."

That same year, Margie had a guest, a young handsome man who loved to go running at dawn. On one particular occasion, he came in from his run a bit curious. "Has anyone ever mentioned a ghost entering the side door?" he asked as he poured himself some coffee. "I saw a beautiful young girl with long brown hair wearing a white peignoir, her hand holding the tail of it close to her waist. She just disappeared into the house."

Margie was taken aback, not quite sure what to say. Since the young guest seemed more curious than bothered by his experience, Margie said, "We've come to love her and live with her. We don't know her story, but she seems quite at home here."

Mama was right about lingering spirits co-existing with the living in some sort of harmony. Mama died before Margie finished her makeover of Doc Kimsey's old house, and her spirit hangs out with me back in our holler. Over time at The Company House, our beautiful young girl spent less and less time walking the halls. I like to think she is happy someone has kept the old place alive, laughter and camaraderie filling its walls again, or maybe she became bored by us all.

SUE WEAVER DUNLAP *lives in Walland, Tennessee, on a mountain farm with her husband Raymond. Publications include* Appalachian Journal, Appalachian Heritage, Pine Mountain

Sand and Gravel, Anthology of Appalachian Writers, Kakalak, and The Southern Poetry Anthology. *Dunlap's works also include* Tuesday's Child, *Main Street Rag, 2025,* A Walk to the Spring House, *Iris Press, 2021,* Knead, *Main Street Rag, 2016, and* Story Tender, *Finishing Line Press, 2014.*

SEVEN
AN ENTITY, AN OUTSIDER
BEREA, KENTUCKY

Susan Tidwell Brown

In August of 1966, I was thrilled to finally arrive at James Hall, a red brick dormitory built in 1918 on the campus of Berea College in Kentucky. My room assignment was on the north end of the second floor with two other students. My best friend, Dee, from Elk Valley, Tennessee, was four doors down the hall. We were elated to be starting our first year of college, even if the curfew was 8 p.m.

That fall, events like the Mountain Day hike went along swimmingly.

Yet a short time later weird happenings began to occur. The initial episode was when Dee said, "Don't think I'm weird but I have to tell you something that is very strange!" She went on to say she was being followed down the long hall at night when she went to the tiled second floor bathroom. There were no sounds except her quiet steps. But she felt an ominous presence stalking her, making her neck prickle in apprehension. "Sometimes, from the corner of my eye, I see a blurry, white form, a bit higher than my waist."

Next, her roommate, Goldie, asked if Dee had been rearranging items in their room. "Why are you drinking my water and moving my toothpaste and Lit notebook under the bed?"

Dee denied doing this.

Then Dee's items were misplaced overnight: a favorite pen, cozy rose blanket and her one precious bottle of French Coty cologne, L'Origan, with the floral fragrance. Her carton of milk was opened and empty.

Goldie denied payback or moving stuff around. Consequently, the two arrived at an understanding—an entity was hard at work on disruption.

I agreed.

At first, the presence felt annoyingly playful. Clothes, washed in the basement wringer washers where Clorox reeked so strongly you could taste it, were dried on strong clotheslines sprawling like spider webs. After all this work, stair climbing, folding, and stacking, we did not take kindly to laundry stacks being knocked over and scattered. Why was this happening? What was going on? It seemed innocuous, mischievous even, but an undercurrent of dread prevailed.

"I might think you were making this up but it's feeling weird in the hall at night," confessed Betty, who lived down the hall.

Dee and I both felt we were being followed up and down the second floor hall, day and night, by the pale presence that appeared whitish and watery around the edges. Dark, strange dreams and nightmares disturbed our sleep. I had night terrors where my mind was fully awake but I couldn't move my body.

"My chest feels like an elephant is sitting on it," Dee said. "I can't move or scream for help."

There were bumping sounds, thuds, feelings of imminent danger. The now-malevolent presence was attacking our psyches.

The air in our dorm felt heavy and smelled like a storm was approaching. The old cream-colored plaster walls were oppressive. Radiators hissed like coiled rattlers as the weather turned frosty.

We tried to ignore the strangeness but it took root like an evil flower waiting to bloom and spread poison all around us. Dee woke up one night to see Goldie, in a trance, standing over and staring down at her. An insidious terror gripped us in the evenings.

We were sleep deprived and moody. After all, we came to college to have fun, get an education, and nab a degree, not to be haunted. Our grades slipped. Dee had trouble waking up in the morning and was late to her work study assignment as an assistant secretary in the college electric office. Goldie had a dropping grade in Art I, plus her supervisor at her job in needlecraft questioned her attention to detail.

We were in a pickle.

"Well, my mom said to just pray about it," Goldie told us.

We did.

One night an overpowering compulsion to go to the library hit me. I had no research paper due, no periodical to consult. Besides, it was a long walk and cold outside. I shivered. My heart pounded. It was like a pulsating cord of energy pulled me. I went down the hall and rapped on Dee's door. Goldie's stereo was pounding out *Fifth Dimension* by The Byrds. We put on warm coats and hightailed it, hurrying under the quadrangle's oak trees until we opened the thick library doors. Guided by that energy, I walked upstairs to the stacks, a whiff of musty books in my nostrils. Dee followed, a puzzled look on her face. I cannot explain this but my fingers knew the correct book, the right story: *The Horla*. My hand grasped a volume of Guy de Maupassant's short stories. I cracked the book and my flesh got goosebumps. So did hers.

The Horla, written in 1887, is the story of a Frenchman's struggle with an entity that entered his home by the sea from a passing Brazilian ship. It was aggravating at first, drinking his water and milk and misplacing objects. The Horla had a whitish, amorphous shape and followed him relentlessly. The atmosphere of his home became unsettling. As events progressed, the *Horla* attempted to take over his mind and control him. He had horrible dreams, night terrors, and premonitions of doom. At the end, he barred the windows and set fire to his house to kill the Horla. The question remained whether or not he did.

The novella explained our evil, evolving companion. After reading the story, we felt the Horla gradually fade away.

"The prayers worked," Goldie said.

Did the entity know we found it out? Did the story send a message of guiding energy? Finally, we could relax and take deep breaths of air that felt calm. Normality returned but these events remain with me today, almost six decades later. My blood runs cold just writing this tale, dredging up the dark memories.

A graduate of Berea College and the University of Tennessee, **SUSAN TIDWELL BROWN** *was born in Jellico, Tennessee, to a family of prescient mountain people. She was raised in Highcliff, Tennessee; Williamsburg, Kentucky; and Norwood, Ohio. An educator, she worked many years in public schools. Her most enjoyable years were as a school psychologist and high school counselor. She wrote for* The Berea Citizen, Jellico Community Voice, *and the* London Sentinel-Echo. *Recently, one of her poems was published in* These Mosaics *by Hindman Settlement School. From childhood, she has been connected to creative, universal energy.*

— EIGHT —
A VISIT FROM THE MAYOR

KNOXVILLE, TENNESSEE

Suzy Trotta

I have never seen a ghost, but I have heard several. I grew up in a house with footsteps in rooms no one walked through and where a woman told me good night, though no woman was there. I've been in homes where doors closed for no apparent reason, and footsteps followed me across rooms. So when we bought a house built in 1925, you would think I might have wondered if it had ghosts. But I don't think like a normal person.

I originally went to list the house, being a real estate agent, and immediately decided to buy it. I'm not a spontaneous person, but I was on a roll. I had just gotten my first dog as an adult the day before, so I decided to buy a house as well. In a twenty-year real estate career, I've been in thousands of homes and for reasons I can't explain, fell in love with this one. I'm still in love with it. I didn't care about its history or anything else. I just want to live here for a really long time.

The house is a two-story brick craftsman with a wide front porch, a port cochère, hardwood floors throughout, high ceilings and lots of natural light. I grew up in an old home and it reminded me of that.

It was my friend Penny who looked up its history and told me the house had been built by a former mayor of Knoxville, Erastus Eugene Patton. With a name like that, it was maybe understandable he went by E.E. Patton. She did a little background on Erastus. He built the house before he was mayor in 1945 and only lived there a few years, perhaps due to the Great Depression. At any rate, he didn't seem to have been a very exciting historical figure. I thought it was cool that a mayor built our house, but I didn't think much else about him.

We moved in with our then four-month-old dog and started the business of unpacking and getting to know the neighbors. Unlike my old neighborhood, all the way over in Tony West Knoxville, this new neighborhood called "Parkridge" or "Park City"-depending on whom you talk to or how much of a fight you want to get into-was close-knit, perhaps because it was in the process of transitioning. The house I bought had been vacant for years after being foreclosed on, and the previous owner bought it for a song and completely renovated it.

This renovation included finishing formerly unused attic space into an enormous master suite, complete with an anteroom that would become my sewing room. This room has become a sanctuary. Every night when I go to bed, I think how much I love our enormous bedroom with its high ceilings, dark navy walls, and comfy bed.

My house may have been a sanctuary, but my new neighborhood was a minefield. To say I was unprepared for the personalities and drama was an understatement. Also, this neighborhood had its own Facebook page, and people were not shy about posting. There were a lot of "gunshots or fireworks?" posts around certain holidays and other posts just asking if anyone had a cup of sugar they could borrow. Someone's always available to help, and that's one of the reasons I still love most of my neighbors all these years later.

The "gunshots or fireworks" question was frequent during my early years in Parkridge. It wasn't uncommon for someone to post on the Facebook page that they had either seen or heard gunfire on their street and for neighbors to track drive-by shooters or other illegal activity in real time. It might sound strange, but none of this violence really bothered me. It all seemed diaphanous, like it was happening around me, but not really happening to me. It was hazy and unreal. Plus, I had a husband and a dog to protect me. What could go wrong?

Sometime after we moved in, I checked Facebook before bed one night, after hearing what I assumed were gunshots. Sure enough, someone reported hearing the same thing several blocks away and had even seen someone running from the scene.

Cocooned in my delusion of safety, I turned my phone off and snuggled into bed with a good book beside my sleeping husband and puppy.

That is until I heard the first door slam.

I sat straight up in bed, looking around to see what had happened, thinking I would see my husband also sitting up and maybe my dog as well. No one was awake but me. In fact, both of my bedmates were snoring softly without a care in the world. How had they just slept through that?

My heart raced as I tried to figure out what happened.

I had no doubt I heard a door slam. It was somewhere out on the second-floor landing. Four possible doors could have slammed: three bedrooms and a bathroom. By my keen powers of observation, I deduced the door to our bedroom hadn't slammed because it was still open. (All that Agatha Christie I read as a child paid off.)

Though I could have investigated further, I decided staying in my bed, safe with my loved ones, was a better choice. Maybe I had heard something outside or maybe I was just freaking myself out. After all, my dog hadn't even woken up and weren't dogs supposed to be keenly aware of things we can't even hear, see, or smell?

With this comforting thought, I laid back down to continue reading.

That's when another door slammed.

I say another, but for all I know, it could have been the same door. Either way, I sat back up again, now one hundred percent sure my husband and dog would be awake.

They were not.

There was no one else in the house. I wasn't concerned about an intruder. I was concerned about having a goddamn ghost in my new dream home. Not knowing what else to do and tired of these shenanigans, I shouted, "This is our house now, Erastus! Cut it out!"

To this day I don't know why I pegged Mayor Patton as the guilty party, but that's the first thing that came to mind. At any rate, my pronouncement didn't wake up anyone else in the bedroom, and I was starting to wonder what even could, so I sat for a few minutes to see if I would get any kind of response. When I didn't, I finished reading and fell asleep.

The next morning, I woke up and took my coffee out to my new front porch to enjoy the mild weather. As I looked out over my new yard, I saw something that didn't belong there: a shotgun. Or what I thought looked like a shotgun.

I went back in the house and got my husband, who confirmed it was indeed a shotgun. Remembering the Facebook posts, I told him about the shots fired a few streets up. While he called the police to report the gun, I went back on the neighborhood page to see what had happened in the night.

It turned out a lot had happened. While I was trying to read and yelling at ghosts, my more vigilant neighbors were tracking the shooter from four streets away right to our very street and block, right about the time that first door slammed.

I sat for a minute, trying to think this through. Was it possible whoever or whatever had slammed those doors had been trying to warn us of an armed man running toward our yard? Could the ghost of a former mayor of Knoxville have been trying to protect me?

To this day, I have no idea. But I do know two things: those doors slammed, and nothing even slightly ghostly has ever happened in our home again.

I told my husband all about this. Having had his own experiences with the disembodied, he didn't laugh. He knows there are more things in heaven and earth than we know a damn thing about.

And I don't know that it was Erastus who slammed the doors that night or why I told him to stop. But not wanting to seem ungrateful, just in case we ever needed him again, I stood on the landing the next night after my husband and dog went to bed and thanked a ghost I had heard and would never see for his service.

SUZY TROTTA *is the author of* Open House: Mostly True Tales of Crazy in Southern Real Estate. *The twenty-year real estate veteran has also had work published in The Knoxville Writers Guild's* ReView, *the online news magazine* Compass, *and the book* Seven Secrets to the Perfect Personal Essay. *You can read her other ghost stories in* 23 Tales: Appalachian Ghost Stories, Legends & Other Mysteries *and* 24 Tales: More Appalachian Ghost Stories, Legends & Mysteries. *Suzy lives in Knoxville, Tennessee, with her husband, cats, and her dog, Jolene.*

NINE
Thru the Night
The Long Trail, Vermont

Annika Ringen

The Long Trail is the oldest continuous footpath in the United States. At 272 miles, it follows the main ridge of the Green Mountains from the Massachusetts-Vermont line to the Canadian border. Each year, hundreds of thru hikers set out to complete the trail in one go.

~ Green Mountain Club

06/29/2022
Day 16

A deep, heavy fog settled down on the forest as dusk wrung out the last light of day. I had paced today's hike well, getting into camp with ample time to eat, change, and journal by natural light. But my ease slipped away as the world dimmed around me. I was a captive to the darkness leaking in through gaps between hardwoods, circling the three-sided shelter and enclosing me within.

That familiar fear of mine ran deep like the roots of an old oak, and I didn't know why. I just obeyed, tucking my lower half tight into my sleeping bag, even if I would be awake awhile longer.

I thought through this experience I might have outgrown my childhood phobia. For sixteen days I had been solo thru-hiking Vermont's Long Trail, headed north for Canada. Everything I needed was strapped to my back and carried up and over each peak and down and through every notch of the Green Mountain's rocky spine. I had walked through swollen knees, bent through aching hips, hauled my pack on welts the size of grapes, stepped with damp and shriveled feet. Whether pouring rain or beating sun, I continued along the rugged footpath. But no matter how fast or far or strong I hiked, I could not outpace that fear. It crept up like a tiny mosquito buzzing in my ear: *zip up your sleeping bag, tuck in your arms, hide away from what lurks in the shadows.*

The nights were easier with other hikers around. There weren't as many since I started on the more remote, northern parts of the trail. Tonight, however, the shelter was packed, even more so than usual with the oncoming rain. There were two girls, a year younger than me and attending my college. Part of me envied how they had each other's company as they snuck out for a joint behind the shelter. I stayed, stretching my tight calves within my sleeping bag, and let myself think how they must not fear a night in an empty shelter. As was the case at many of the shelters I've stayed in, there were several male solo thru hikers, but I was the only female.

Then she appeared. Her figure seemed to be made of the mist itself as she drifted in from the dark woods. Slender like a birch tree, she had pale skin and a patchwork of tattoos that created a gallery around her arms and legs. As she came closer, I saw she was familiar.

I had seen her only yesterday. She passed me on the steep descent into Smugglers Notch, the most exaggerated elevation change of the entire hike. And she was cruising. I figured she'd be miles ahead of me by now. I learned she was headed down and into town and that the promise of pizza might have put an extra spring in her step. Still, if she left town this morning that meant she put up a seventeen-mile day today and on some hard terrain. That's fast.

Like a spider spinning her web, the tattooed hiker quietly, so quietly, made her bed in the last corner of space on the shelter floor. She put down her sleeping bag straight on the wooden boards, noting she was usually a hammock sleeper if not for the rain, hence the lack of sleeping pad. I pictured her in that suspended state and found myself in awe of her contentment to be alone, the trees her only company and, on a clear night, the forest canopy her only roof.

I smelt the rain before I heard it. Then, sure enough, came the tap tap tap on the shelter roof. It seemed the tattooed hiker had got in just in time, as if the forest held its thirst until its friend could make it to a dry place.

Though we had only just met, the lot of us were huddled together under the shelter roof like a pack of dogs, not a lick of floor board separating our patchwork of sleeping bags. We did learn each others' names, trail names that is, as the night deepened. A trail name, either bestowed or chosen, alluded to some part of your experience on trail, which came in handy as you try to recall the many new people you've met. Effectively, I could not forget, even if I wanted to, the two girls around my age who make up the duo Happy Feet and Party Pisser. And I wondered if it was a reference to her pale complexion or something else entirely when the tattooed hiker introduced herself as Ghost.

It was only when the rain was too loud to talk over that we put our heads down to rest, and I was thankful for the sound drowning out my fear and ushering me into a deep sleep.

06/30/2022
Day 17

I was one of the first up and out of camp in the morning. That was typical. At the earliest light I stirred, wanting to give myself plenty of day to work with. When I made to leave camp, I looked one more time to Ghost, who seemed nowhere close to being on her way. The contents of her backpack still made a small mess in the back corner of the shelter where she'd slept, and she took unhurried bites of a breakfast. She was quick enough, though, that

I knew she'd catch up to and pass me at some point today, maybe even within the first few miles.

The day's hike began with a climb. It was about three miles to summit, and just before, a massive slab of rock, at least twice my height, protruded from the damp earth. The trail passed right alongside it. The imposing stone wall slanted down and away from the path, posing like it could tip over at any time. Rivulets ran down channels in the rock then dripped off when the slope became too inverted, creating a glistening beaded curtain of dew. Had the morning not still had a chill, I would have stood beneath it. At the very least, I tipped my head back to wet my curls, which were tied back in their usual braids.

The Long Trail was notoriously wet, and today was no exception. Though I had dried my shoes and socks out in the midday sun only yesterday, they were already soaked. There was little choice when stepping stones fell away and mud was the only way to walk through. At times, seas of thriving ferns, some as tall as my hip, stretched endlessly across the forest, parting just enough to indicate a trail. As you passed by, they'd paint your legs like dozens of water color brushes. But at least water is in no short supply.

I arrived at camp by early afternoon. The day was still plenty young, and I was on the shorter side of my usual mileage, but the next shelter was far enough away that I didn't wish to push on farther.

The campground was wide and open. On one end was a four-sided shelter, and the other fell off over a striking ledge. I took up a spot near the north-facing overlook to eat and stretch. Fat, white clouds cast shadows over spots of the valley below and up the side of the mountain rising beyond. I surveyed its grandness and compared it to my map, which gave more details about its long, sustained ascent. I found myself more content with my decision to camp here considering the next shelter was up and over the other side of my current view.

I turned at the sound of snapping sticks.

"Sorry, I didn't mean to startle you," she said.

A woman, a decade or two older than myself, trekked over toward the ledge, her dark, curly ponytail bobbing with each crunching step. She must have been able to tell I was a thru hiker—unfortunately for her, it was likely due to my odor— because she said:"You're probably so used to being in the quiet by yourself, I should leave you to it." She went on in her bubbly way about how she was only out for a few nights, this being the first. In truth, it was a relief to have someone else there with me at the shelter.

Perhaps I spoke too soon, because then, what must have been over a dozen girls in their early teens came one by one into the campsite, like marching ants. Lucky for me they went right to work assembling tent poles and staking corners into the ground. By the looks of it, we would not all have fit in the shelter. I hadn't actually been inside the little cabin yet, but with the campground suddenly teaming, I headed in that direction to claim a spot.

The shelter had two bunk platforms, one over top the other, that stretched the length of it. I rolled out my sleeping bag onto a far side of the lower bunk. Before too long I was joined by Happy Feet and Party Pisser. Today was their longest day on the trail so far, and they came into camp sweaty and hungry. As they made dinner, they mentioned taking a more leisurely hike tomorrow and exploring a swimming hole they spotted on the map. If it had taken them most of the day to get here, I had to ask.

"Did you guys see Ghost today?"

This campsite was a little bit off the trail. Maybe she had gone by sometime after I got here and hiked on to the next shelter.

"No," one of them said.

"I thought she would have passed me," I said.

"We thought she'd pass us. When we left camp this morning she was still there."

Panic grew through me like a gnarly weed. They left before her and she never caught up. There was no reason to stop between last night's camp and here. No grocery store, no hostel, no town. Even if there was, Ghost just stopped in town two nights ago. I checked my phone for service, wondering who I could even contact to report a missing hiker. When I finally looked up, one of the girls had opened the shelter's logbook. Steadily, as if convincing herself of the words as they crossed her tongue, she read:

"*Stopped in for a little bit to nap. Itching to finish, so I'm going back out to hike through the night.*"

~ *Ghost*

ANNIKA RINGEN *works as a producer and editor for a Vermont Access Network media center that serves central Vermont. Whether for screen, stage, or page, her work explores nature, humor, and the human experience. She is fueled by time spent outside and enjoys recreating in every season with her partner Cal and her dog Polly.*

TEN

ELIZABETH

LEBANON, VIRGINIA

Brandon Whited

A young lady admitted to Russell County Hospital found herself unable to sleep as a result of her medication, so she spent that night sitting up in bed watching television. It was busy on the floor, and she frequently saw her assigned nurse running to and from the supply closet, trailed by an older lady in a white gown who perhaps suffered from dementia. When the nurse came into the young lady's room alone the next morning, the young lady asked about the woman in the white gown who had followed the nurse around all night. The nurse was shaken by the question. She had neither seen nor heard the white-gowned lady the entire night, nor had any of her coworkers.

The resident hospital ghost in rural Lebanon, Virginia, has become something of a friend to the employees, an experience with the specter being a rite-of-passage for new hires. Said to be the wife of one of the hospital's earliest physicians, her name is Elizabeth, though no one can recall her last name. An older lady, she breathed her last in Room 7 of what is now the Clearview Psychiatric Unit, which at the time still served as part of the medical wing. Elizabeth's cause of death is unknown, as is the date of her passing. The nearest approximation is that it occurred sometime in the 1960s.

How much of Elizabeth's biography is apocryphal will remain a source of conjecture, but to a number of longtime employees her spectral form is without doubt real. While I never personally encountered her during my twelve years of employment at the hospital as a licensed practical nurse, I worked with many who were certain they had.

Elizabeth most often appears at night on the psychiatric ward where she is said to have died. Be it an employee or patient who saw her, their description of the ghost never varied: an older lady wearing a white gown. Most witnesses see her as a full-bodied apparition, appearing corporeal, not translucent or glowing.

One night a part-time employee on the psychiatric ward had a particularly frightening run-in with the ghost. This nurse normally worked at the state mental institution. A broad, towering man, he didn't scare easily. Nevertheless, when he entered the ward's closet-sized medication room on the night in question and was confronted by the sight of Elizabeth's ghost standing before him, the gentle giant was nearly inconsolable. For the remainder of his overnight shift another nurse had to escort him in and out of the medication room.

Another night, a different psychiatric nurse was performing the room checks required to be carried out every fifteen minutes on high-risk patients. When she passed the infamous Room 7, she could see by the limited hallway light a lady sitting on the end of one of the beds. Asked if she needed anything, the figure replied simply, "No." The nurse made it to the end of the hallway before it dawned on her that Room 7 was supposed to be unoccupied. She hurried back to the room, only to find it empty.

Sightings of the ghost aren't limited to the psychiatric unit. On a rare quiet night on one of the medical floors, a level-headed nursing supervisor was seated alone at the nurses' station, spending the early morning quietly reviewing paperwork. Suddenly, movement caught her eye. An older lady wearing a white gown casually walked down the hallway past the desk, heading toward the elevators. In the seconds it took the supervisor to rise and look around the corner of the station, the lady had vanished. No patient admitted to that floor fit the woman's description, and visiting hours had ended many hours earlier.

In at least one instance, Elizabeth proved to be helpful. One evening, while the day shift gave its report to the oncoming night shift, an elderly gentleman rang his call bell and asked for a cup of coffee. It was some time before anyone could fulfill his request, but when they did, they were surprised to find that he already had a fresh cup of coffee sitting on his bedside table. When asked how he had already obtained his coffee, the gentleman calmly explained that an older lady in a white gown had brought it to him. This patient was perfectly lucid and unfamiliar with the hospital's haunted history. Adding further to the supernatural aspect of the episode, the only coffee pot on this floor was in the room where the day shift was meeting with their night-shift counterparts.

BRANDON WHITED *is an author of historical nonfiction specializing in the Titanic disaster and general maritime history. He serves as a trustee of Titanic International Society and has provided input and consulted for* The Washington Post *and* Netflix. *His most recent book,* Southwest Virginia and Maritime Disasters: From the SS Vestris to the Morro Castle and Beyond, *was released by Arcadia Publishing in 2024.*

ELEVEN
THE BROKEN STONE OF HOPEFUL CARTER

SUNBRIGHT, TENNESSEE

Patty Ireland

I like old cemeteries. It's weird, I know, but I've had an infatuation with them since childhood. I've spent many an afternoon wandering off down some overgrown path through woods and fields to find a gathering of abandoned stones, gray and collapsed, and "chalk" them in order to learn who lies beneath.

Once my brother and I did this together in a little church cemetery off a country road in New Hampshire. We were both old souls, born poets who liked to think as far as we could think, to ponder and question and dare God. We began noticing that a good number of the individuals buried there, who ranged in age from babies to the elderly, died within only a few days of one another.

"Could've been smallpox or typhus," my brother speculated. "Could've been scarlet fever."

That was a golden autumn day back in 1976. We walked among the old stones for a couple of hours, deciphering names and dates, contemplating who was related to whom, and what it might feel like if the rapture happened right then and there, and all those people came popping up out of the ground at once. What would such a hectic scene look like? Would the newly resurrected run smack into each other in their rush to join the Lord in the skies?

Would they recognize each other or simply fly onward toward their lofty destinations? Of course, this discussion led to talk of our own mortality. Did we really believe the literal version of scripture we'd heard being preached from the pulpit as children? Or were we doubting, in some far corner of our minds, the faith of our fathers? Was it all nothing more than a lovely lie invented by humans to make ourselves feel a little better about the brutal truth? Little did I know that my brother would die from a massive heart attack sixteen years later, almost to the day.

I don't often go to my brother's grave or to the graves of my parents or my other brother, who also died young from a heart attack, or to the grave of the sibling I never knew who died years before I was born. I don't often visit the graves of my grandparents or my aunts and uncles or my best friend from first grade who passed suddenly with MRSA. Why? It certainly isn't for the lack of loving them. Perhaps it's because I feel sad for those whose names and stories have faded. Or maybe it's because those more modern graveyards seem sterile and commercialized with their mausoleums, minimalist style architecture, battery-powered grave lamps, and plastic flowers. Give me a wild field. I'm more at home there.

Which leads me to today. I'm off walking on a friend's land near Sunbright, Tennessee, where I've heard there is an old cemetery, so old that the stones are all faded and fallen, so old that the wrought-iron fence that once surrounded the cemetery is now rusted and torn down by cows that meander about. So old that nobody knows anything about it and nobody takes care of it. Ever. Just my cup of tea.

I'm older now too. More enlightened. Closer to my own return to the ground. I have now learned that traditional tombstone rubbing methods like chalking are actually harmful to the stones. They will eventually wear away the carvings altogether, leading to flaking and breaking. So, I no longer come equipped with chalk, a wire brush, and paper. Today I come prepared to use the more historically conscious "foil method" in which a thin sheet of aluminum foil is placed against the stone. A light-weight makeup brush is then pressed into the foil to expose lettering. I also bring along a mirror. The idea here is that if the foil method fails, I can cast sunlight from the mirror onto the surface of the stone from an angle so that the engraving reveals a shadow, making it readable.

I follow my friend's directions through a shaded wood, down into a ravine, over a small creek, and into an open area of fields. Several cows are mulling about. They turn, their large eyes blinking slowly. I speak gently to them, knowing they will all be sent for slaughter soon. They walk away from me at first, but I keep telling them silly, tender lies like "It's okay. It will be all right." They turn their massive heads back toward me and low softly. I am moved by the sound of their innocence.

Suddenly, my right foot hits something hard. I swear a little, look down and then feel glad, despite the pain. For, there is my first stone. It is a footstone pointing east, facing Jesus and the rising sun. I look west, parting the field grass with my hands, to find the headstone. While the cows watch me curiously, I drop my gear and lay my hands on the rough-edged marker as if to bless it somehow.

It isn't long before I uncover an unusual name: Lyre Carter. In a few more minutes, I have a title for a true life story: "Consort of William Carter." I have learned over the years that in the 17th through the 19th centuries, this term would have meant that Lyre Carter was William's wife who preceded him in death. I now uncover firm dates that mark a beginning and an ending: "Born 20 July in the Year of Our Lord 1778. Died 30 December in the Year of Our Lord 1794." Next, I spot a single word, spelled all in capital letters: MOTHER. I let the words roll around in my head and settle: This young girl, who passed at the tender age of sixteen, was someone's wife, someone's mother.

Knowing that Lyre Carter's Husband will likely lie to the right of his wife since her headstone faces east, I begin searching for him. I have learned through my research a theory that accounts for this tradition: husbands wanted their wives buried closest to their hearts, which meant she would lie to his left. This placement is also a reflection of a couple's wedding day since the man traditionally stands to the right of his bride.

Oddly enough, William Carter's stone is nowhere to be found. Instead, I begin uncovering other stones that date from the late 1700s to the 1850s, some of which also bear the name "Carter," though I can't determine any relationship between Lyre and the others.

Shading my eyes from the harsh sun, I spot remnants of the old wrought iron fence. I am able to trace its path, to see where the parameters of the cemetery were initially drawn. I step over the fallen, rusted remnants of the fence. Clearly, their spiraling scroll work was at one time intricate and beautiful. I come upon what was once the gate and can see that the shape of an ornate cross is welded into the middle of each gateway.

As I take a moment to look outward, I notice something protruding from the windblown grass about twenty-five feet outside the gates; it is another stone, small and lonely among the music of breezes and bird chatter. I gather my things, walk over to the spot and set to work at once, curious to know whose name is engraved there and how this tombstone wound up so far away from the others. As I bend down to inspect it, I see that the stone is broken into two large pieces with smaller, cracked chips lying nearby. Still, I am determined to learn all I can about the poor person who lies beneath.

In a few moments, I once more have success with the foil method. An ironic, all things considered, name appears on the larger piece of stone: "Hopeful." Then I see the last name coming through on a broken remnant lying nearby: Carter. In smaller lettering, the word "Daughter" emerges beneath. Next are ominous dates I find on the second, larger portion of the stone: "Born and Departed This Life, 30 December, 1794." I dash quickly back to Lyre's grave to check the dates on her stone. Now Lyre's sad story takes shape for me. At sixteen years old, she gave birth to a daughter. She obviously died doing so, I surmise, and then, tragically, her little girl died too. A stillbirth, perhaps?

Finally, the foil reveals a last comment that triggers a lingering thought that burns a big hole in my chest: "Resting in God's Arms." Is little Hopeful resting in heaven? Is she resting here beneath a broken stone far out beyond the fallen cemetery gates right now? Is she resting anywhere? Does the consciousness that was Hopeful Carter remain in existence in any form at all? Or is she nothing more than a pile of bleached bones whose little wooden box disintegrated around her over two centuries ago, just eleven years after the Revolutionary War ended?

I am so stirred by learning these secrets of the stones that I suddenly feel utterly exhausted. My head spins, light and surreal. My hands are shaking. I look at my arms; they are red with sunburn. How long have I been out here in the hot sun? I glance at my watch. In my zeal to learn about the abandoned cemetery, it only seems a few minutes, but I can see I've been here now for four hours without drinking water or applying sunscreen. I decide to find some shade and unpack the lunch I've brought along. A little way off, I see a large oak tree with sturdy boughs stretching like protective arms over the rural landscape. I make my way to it unsteadily, sit myself down beneath its cool shadows and dive into my drink and sandwich. The cows I saw earlier are moving slowly, far in the distance now, making their way back to my friend's barn where they think they'll be safe, naïve to the truth that one day soon, they'll be taken away never to return. Sharp flickers of sunlight dance through the fields, occasionally hitting the old stones, lighting them up like glittering specks of gold. The whole scene swirls around me like a dream.

I am halfway through my sandwich, feeling some better, taking a big swig of the cool lemonade in my thermos, when I notice a figure approaching from out of the nearby woods. At first, I think it's my friend coming to check on me. Then I realize this figure is wearing a long dress and some sort of head covering, definitely not my friend's style. As she draws closer, I can see that she is carrying a wide basket. Strands of dark hair protrude from her hat, which now reveals itself to be more like an old-fashioned bonnet. Her dress is pale yellow, as is the hat. She almost glides toward me as she makes her way through the tall field grass.

I stand as she comes nearer. "Hello?" I call.

"Oh, hello there," she replies, smiling as she picks up her skirts and continues toward me.

Probably Amish, I think. Or Mennonite. I know both groups live nearby as Tennessee is a popular destination for "plain" communities.

"Fine day, ain't it?" she asks in her thin, young voice.

"Yes, it is," I respond, looking her up and down. "A little hot out here, though."

"Yes ma'am. That's God's truth," she agrees, bowing her head slightly. "Still, a soul can't complain," she continues. "I'll take these summer days over the snow of a bleak December any time."

I set my sandwich down and put out my right hand. "Patty Ireland," I say.

She tilts her head and looks at me as if perplexed.

I gaze back, equally confused. "My name is Patty Ireland," I explain.

"Oh," she says, "Obliged to make your acquaintance, ma'am." She does a little curtsy, but does not offer her name, nor does she return a hand to my outstretched one. I awkwardly withdraw it.

In her basket are wild flowers. She puts a pale arm up to her forehead, looking out toward the graveyard. "You come for the decoration?" she asks.

"Decoration?"

She turns back toward me, smiling again. I can see that her eyes are clear and blue. One tooth is missing from the bottom of her mouth. "Yes ma'am. The decoration."

I stand there stupidly.

"Of the graveyard yonder," she clarifies.

I know that in outlying rural areas some churches still hold what they called "Decoration Days" during which parishioners come to clean up the grass around tombstones and lay flowers. I can't figure, though, that this small, downtrodden cemetery, which I was told had not been tended in decades, would be part of such a ceremony. "Um, no. I didn't realize there was one," I say.

"Yes ma'am. Every year regular on this day."

"Well, that is a lovely tradition," I remark.

She nods her head and brushes the hair away from one eye. "I brung flowers that I picked special," she says.

"They're beautiful."

"Yes ma'am." She smiles but again eyes me as if uncertain about my presence.

"You're probably wondering why I'm here," I say laughingly, trying to reassure her. "That's because I like old cemeteries. It's strange, I know, but I enjoy discovering them and learning as much as I can. I'm a history buff."

Her brow furrows slightly. "Do you do man's work?" she asks suddenly.

I snicker a little. "Excuse me?"

"No disrespect, ma'am. I just thought maybe you done man's work considering your garments and all."

I give another awkward chuckle. "No. I'm a college professor. I dressed casually today because I knew I'd be out here in the hot sun poking around the old gravestones, you know."

Her frown becomes deeper. "College?"

"Yes, I teach at Pellissippi State in Knoxville."

Her smile fades. "That don't make clear sense. I don't know no such place. And what do you mean 'poking around' at old stones?"

"Oh, I'm sorry," I stutter. "I didn't mean literally poking the stones or the ground. I would never dishonor a graveyard. I just meant that I use methods to try and decipher the lettering on the faded stones, that's all."

Her smile is totally gone now. Her frown is gone, too. Her face becomes stoic. Vacant. "Stones ain't faded," she says coldly. "Graves ain't old."

Not knowing how to respond, I stand silent.

Her voice resumes. "But one of them coffins was moved off away from the others—moved from the care of the one person that loved the remains inside. And then that grave was defaced—spoilt it was. The stone was split in two when a certain bastard-man dropped it down with a thundering of rage. It ain't right."

She begins walking slowly toward the graveyard like a robot. "It ain't right," she continues muttering as she walks on. "Especially for a man who calls himself a faithful husband and father, a man who calls himself a righteous follower of Christ Jesus. It ain't right and that bastard-man needs to pay."

I watch as she moves closer to the small stone remnants outside what were once the gates of the little cemetery. When she reaches it, she bends down.

I now follow her, carefully approaching from behind as she kneels beside the broken stone of little Hopeful Carter.

"Don't matter what color a child's skin might be. Black, white. Don't matter. Can't nobody tell me that If it were your own child, your blood, you ought'n to do what is right. No man has got no right to kill any child, especially his own, just because of what others might speculate." Her mechanical voice softens a little: "Ain't their business no how."

Tenderly, she gathers the flowers from her basket and lays them one by one over the broken stone. When she is done, her thin, high voice resumes its machine-like tone, as if every word was little more than an echo of actual human sound: "It ain't right for a bastard-man to kill his wife and child when he is the one carrying the blood that made the child black in the first place. And it ain't right for him to tell untruths and have his wife and child buried by a preacher proper-like just for show when he's the one murdered both of them in cold blood. And it ain't right for him to come back later on and move the body of his own child out of his family's graveyard and break the stone of his own child. And it sure ain't right for him to go off then and marry up with some other woman and have him another child, a pure white child, that he loves and dotes on."

Finished then, she rises and walks past me, as if I don't exist. Back over the tall grass she treks, carrying the empty basket, lifting her long skirts as she moves, fading, waning, like a grainy scene from an old silent movie being replayed against a glaringly bright screen of field and sky. I watch her until she vanishes into nothingness.

I stand there shaken and dumbfounded. Did this young girl, suffering from some mental illness, wander off from a neighboring Amish community and into my afternoon, or did I pass out? Is this a dream manufactured by my poetic, relentlessly God-defiant mind? Have I been hallucinating due to heat stroke?

I hurriedly gather my things and run breathless back to the veneer of the present, the assumed safety of my friend's modern farmhouse, but I can't bring myself to go inside. I get in my car and take off. I say not one word about any of this to my friend or to anyone else until now. Right now, when I sit down to write this story.

Because I'm still fascinated with old cemeteries. I guess some people never learn.

PATTY IRELAND *is an associate professor of English at Pellissippi State in Knoxville, Tennessee and the founder and director of its annual Young Creative Writer's Workshop. In addition to being a published writer of fiction and poetry, she is an established BMI songwriter. Her stories, creative nonfiction and poems have appeared in* Still: The Journal, *100 Days in Appalachia's* "Creators and Innovators," Cutleaf Journal, Untelling, Appalachia Bare, *and various anthologies, including* 23 Tales: Appalachian Ghost Stories, Legends & Other Mysteries *and* 24 Tales: More Appalachian Ghost Stories, Legends & Mysteries. *She is at work on a memoir and recently completed a novel.*

TWELVE
Ghostly Visit
KINGSTON, TENNESSEE

Patricia Hope

She was young, her beauty indescribable, the way these things usually are. She stood, no, more like floated, on the other side of my window as I stood frozen to the winter floor. I remember thinking she couldn't be real because it was bitterly cold outside on that December night. Her gown floated around her, layers and layers of material thin as butterfly wings. Her face was pale but not white as you'd expect a ghost's to be. Her long hair was brown and full, her expression neither happy nor sad but more like someone sleepwalking. Only seconds passed before my fear worked its way to my vocal cords. Still, I was drawn to the apparition in a strange, fascinating kind of way.

I was ten and visiting my grandparents while school was out for Christmas. We lived in the small East Tennessee community of Swan Pond, where my stepfather took care of a dairy farm, and my mother took care of four kids. As the crow flies, my grandparents weren't very far away, but getting to their farm took two hours around curvy backroads and along the river's edge. Still, my stepfather said I could visit with them until Christmas Eve. Then he and Mom would pick me up so I'd be home with them for Christmas.

When I told my grandparents what I'd seen through the window, they went out onto the porch, coaxed me to come see there was no one there before the chill hurried us back to the fireside. A blanket over the window and I could finally lie in my bed listening to my grandparents talk through the wall. The walls were thin in the old farmhouse where they lived, a house they had inherited some forty years earlier. It was one of my favorite places to be most of the time, but tonight I was scared.

"Maybe the story is true, Henry," my grandmother said softly as I strained to listen.

"Naw, it's just an old house," Grandpa said. "The moonlight was playing tricks on the window. Paw was just trying to scare you women with that story."

"But he said she died here, giving birth to your Uncle Raymond. Only she kept coming back to see her child. He said she couldn't rest in peace."

"Yeah, but nobody saw her after they moved away from this old place."

"A spirit can't depart the place where it dies until it finds peace. You know that."

"That's an ole wives' tale, Mollie. Anyway, what would she want around here after all these years? Raymond's done died, too. That's why we're living here, remember? He left it to us. Believe me, only poor human folks with no choice would live here." He turned to humor as he always did. "No haint would be caught dead here, especially on a cold winter night."

"Henry, quit making fun. Maybe she doesn't know he died. Maybe she's there every night and we don't know it."

"All I know is she's not there now. Let's go to bed. You don't need to be scaring the girl with all them tales."

I could hear him stoke the fire, lay another log against the chill that was sure to get worse in the night to come. The big iron bed in the corner of the living room creaked with his weight. Long after their peaceful sleep filled the house, I huddled under my blankets and listened as boards creaked and wind serenaded the night.

    I never saw her again. My grandmother would tell me years later her name was Ethel, but the next morning, I watched from my window as Grandpa showed Grandma two sets of footprints made by bare feet on frosty grass … one small, as if made by a small delicate woman, the other dug deep, as if from a grown man.

PATRICIA HOPE's *writing has appeared in* 23 Tales Appalachian Ghost Stories, Legends & Other Mysteries, *the* Anthology of Appalachian Writers, MockingHeart Review, Artemis, *Guideposts'* Blessed by His Love, Chicken Soup for the Soul, Bluebird Word, Pigeon Parade Quarterly, The Mildred Haun Review, Liquid Imagination, American Diversity Report, *and many others. She lives in Oak Ridge, Tennessee.*

THIRTEEN
ECHOES OF THE UNSEEN
WASHINGTON COUNTY, VIRGINIA

Ronda L. Caudill

Growing up as a medium in my family was difficult, especially because of the places we lived. In rural Washington County, Virginia, I spent my childhood in several haunted houses. My parents rented, and since money was tight, the homes we lived in were always old—some with long histories, others with secrets they kept hidden until we were already inside. These houses became the driving force behind my development as a medium. I was open to a world not everyone could experience. While many members of my extended family had ghostly encounters, they lacked the gift—or curse—of communicating with those on the other side. That burden was mine alone to bear, and these experiences shaped the medium I was destined to become.

One of those houses was a two-story home built in the early 1900s. Compared to some of the others we had lived in, this one was practically young. It stood along Route 91 in Glade Spring, Virginia, its outward appearance giving no hint of what lurked within. I had already experienced my share of strange and unexplainable things over the years, but nothing—nothing—could have prepared me for what was to come.

And it wasn't just me—my entire family came to know the fear that house could instill. The unease settled over us like a heavy fog, creeping into every corner of our lives. Strange noises in the night, shadows that moved without explanation, and the overwhelming feeling of being watched became part of our daily existence.

But I was the only one who, with much regret, attempted to understand the hauntings by trying to connect with whatever lurked inside. I had never known such relentless fear, yet something inside me needed to make sense of it. If I could understand the unseen, perhaps I could find a way to make it leave us alone. But the deeper I reached into that darkness, the more it tightened its grip.

The year was 1981. I was thirteen. My sister was eleven. My brother was seven. My youngest brother wouldn't be born for another three years.

From the outside, the house looked entirely ordinary. A typical two-story structure with dormer windows in the front, a partially enclosed back porch, a pantry, and a sprawling front porch. Inside, there were four bedrooms, a kitchen, a living room, a bathroom, and a laundry room. The hardwood floors creaked underfoot, the plaster walls held the whispers of time, and an old oil furnace rumbled through the nights with a low, steady hum that had an oddly soothing effect.

In the summers, we slept with the windows open, letting the chirps of crickets and the hum of night bugs lull us to sleep. The house was spacious—big enough that, for the first time in my life, I had my own bedroom. No more sharing with my sister.

At first, I was thrilled. That excitement wouldn't last.

The first year in the house was uneventful—actually, it was peaceful. But that peace was deceptive.

The haunting began subtly, creeping into our lives so slowly that we barely noticed at first. A soft knock here. A distant creak there. Something small would fall from a shelf without reason. All little things. All easily explained away.

Until they weren't.

The haunting experiences grew slowly over the course of the next four years. Beginning small and almost unnoticeable. A feeling of being watched. Shadows shifting just out of sight. Strange noises. And then—unmistakable figures.

The first undeniable experience happened in early May of 1982. I was lying on my side in my bed, doing my homework. Now, I should mention that by this time, my brother—who was eight—had earned a reputation for trying to scare my sister and me. My bedroom was at the top of the stairs, open to the staircase with no door to separate the two.

That afternoon, I heard the stair steps creak as if someone were sneaking up. Then, the floorboards in my room groaned under what sounded like careful footsteps.

I looked up just in time to see someone dive onto the floor at the foot of my bed. I was certain it was my brother.

Determined to turn the tables before he could jump out and scare me, I slowly inched my way down the bed, making sure not to let the mattress creak. When I got to the foot, I sprang up on my knees and yelled, "Gotcha!"

The room was empty. No one was there.

A cold, paralyzing terror washed over me. My breath caught in my throat. My heart pounded.

I launched off my bed and flew down the stairs, hitting every other step, until I reached the living room—where I found my brother watching cartoons, completely oblivious.

For weeks, I refused to go upstairs alone.

It was in this house that I began experiencing sleep paralysis—what many call "the old hag syndrome." It started soon after the incident at the foot of my bed. My sister had her own encounters. My brother, too. Even my parents.

One night, my parents were jolted awake by the unmistakable

sound of furniture crashing to the floor. Their first thought was my sister's antique wardrobe, massive and heavy, had tipped over. It could have seriously hurt someone. They rushed upstairs, only to find us all sound asleep. Nothing was out of place.

The ghostly experiences were intensifying, and I felt like I couldn't take any more. Frustration boiled inside me, turning my fear into anger. This was the moment my mediumship truly began to develop. I decided I had to try to communicate with whatever was tormenting us—to make it leave us in peace.

I lit a candle, just as I had seen in countless horror movies. Fighting back the fear and ignoring every shred of better judgment, I called it out. I demanded to know what it wanted and why it wouldn't leave us alone.

That's when I saw it—the dark figure I had once mistaken for my brother. It loomed over me like a living shadow, suffocating the space around me. I was paralyzed with fear, unable to move, unable to breathe. And then, I heard it. A voice echoed in my mind, cold and unwavering: *"This is my house. I am not leaving."*

With every ounce of willpower, I forced my body to move, bolting down the stairs and out into the yard—out of that house where it couldn't follow. I couldn't stand being in that house any longer. Desperate for an escape, I began staying with an elderly woman who needed a caretaker. But peace wouldn't find me there either—her house had its own ghosts. But that's a story for another night.

From that night on, the activity intensified. It centered on the second floor—on us, the kids. My brother was the first to abandon his bedroom, moving to the couch downstairs. My sister and I soon followed. I stopped looking toward the top of the stairs altogether, because every time I did, I saw it—that massive, shadowy figure standing in my room. I was the only one to ever see the shadowy figure.

By this point, I avoided the stairs at all costs, especially at night. I started walking through the laundry room just to avoid walking past them.

Even the bathroom became a problem. The staircase separated it from the kitchen, and I dreaded crossing that invisible line.

By the time my youngest brother was born, the three of us older kids had all moved into the living room—sleeping on the couch and cots. My parents and baby brother slept in the bedroom next to the living room. We were close by. Safety in numbers. Safe from the evil that resided upstairs. We all knew it was a matter of time before it expanded its territory and came downstairs.

That's when the heavy stomping of boots began. Every night, as soon as the sun set, we would hear them. Heavy, methodical footsteps stomping up and down the stairs.

None of us would move. None of us would go to the bathroom. Once we were settled into our "safe area," that's where we stayed.

The stomping continued until dawn. For six months.

Finally, my parents found another house to rent. It was smaller. It had an outhouse. But we didn't care. We were getting out.

Not long after we moved out, we learned that a man had died in that house years ago—his body left undiscovered for days. Whether it was his presence or something far older, I can't say, but even now, that house haunts me. I still have horrific nightmares about being trapped in that house with the evil that lurked within.

The new house was different. Quieter. At least, for everyone else. For me, it was just another chapter.

My sister loved clowns. I have always *hated* clowns. Since we were sharing a room again, I had to deal with her clown collection—mostly figurines. One, in particular, unnerved me. It was mounted inside a silver circle attached to a stand, allowing it to rock back and forth—but only if deliberately pushed. It made a distinct sound when it moved. And of course, she kept it on the dresser at the foot of my bed.

One night, I woke up to that unmistakable rocking sound. I turned my head toward it—my stomach tightening, my breath hitching. The clown was rocking. Violently.

I scrambled out of my bed and dove under my sister's covers, wedging myself between her and the wall, too afraid to move. The next day, I refused to sleep in that room until my mother made my sister put the clown in a drawer.

But the house wasn't done with me yet.

My baby brother was about a year old and often a fretful sleeper. At this stage, he still didn't sleep through the night. Our bedroom was next to the living room, and every night, like clockwork, I would hear my mother get up, prepare his bottle, and rock him back to sleep. The entire process never took more than 20 minutes.

One night, I woke to the familiar sound of the rocking chair creaking rhythmically in the living room. At first, I thought nothing of it—just my mother soothing my baby brother as usual. But as I lay there, eyes still heavy with sleep, I slowly became aware that something wasn't right. I hadn't heard her get up. I hadn't heard my baby brother fussing.

Still, the chair rocked.

I listened, waiting for it to stop, expecting at any moment to hear my mother moving around, but the steady creaking continued. Ten minutes passed. Then twenty. Then forty-five. A sense of unease settled over me. *Why was it taking so long? Was something wrong with my baby brother?*

My pulse quickened as I slipped quietly out of bed, careful not to wake anyone in the house. Moving as silently as I could, I stepped just inside the doorway to the living room. And there it was. The rocking chair swayed back and forth in slow, deliberate motions—*but no one was in it.*

A wave of cold terror washed over me, freezing me in place. My breath caught in my throat as I stared, unable to look away. The chair creaked with every movement, steady and unrelenting, as if an unseen force were sitting there, rocking itself into the night.

Even now, as I write this, chills crawl down my spine.

I stood there for what felt like an eternity, my body locked in place, my mind struggling to comprehend what I was seeing. The only thing louder than the creaking of the chair was the sound of my own heartbeat hammering in my ears.

Then, finally, I gathered the courage to make a mad dash past the chair. I ran like I had never run before, my feet barely touching the floor as I sprinted toward my mother's bedroom. But as I passed the rocking chair, it stopped—*abruptly, unnaturally, as if it knew I was there.*

I didn't stop. I crashed into my mother's room, breathless and trembling, shaking her awake as I frantically told her what I had seen. She walked me back to my room, trying to calm me, but there was no comfort to be found. That night, I refused to sleep alone. I climbed into bed with my sister once again, pressing myself tightly between her and the wall.

Unlike before, I could still see into the living room. I could still see *the chair.*

Once again, I yanked the blanket over my head and cowered for the rest of the night, too afraid to look, too afraid to move.

Thank God I only had a couple of months left before I moved out and into my own apartment. I don't think I could have lasted much longer in that house. My family stayed there for a few more years, but strangely, no one else ever experienced anything unusual.

It was only me.

As I grew older and deepened my understanding of the paranormal, my fear slowly gave way to curiosity. My mediumship flourished—I learned how to forge and sever connections, how to listen, communicate, and decipher the needs of the unseen. In time, I realized this gift wasn't just mine to bear—it had a purpose. I could use it to bring comfort to others, to help those grieving find closure, offering solace to both the living and the dead. But not every spirit seeks peace. Some exist only to unsettle, to frighten, to torment. And despite all I've learned, there are still times when the presence of something truly dark sends me running—out of houses, into the night—desperate to escape whatever lurks in the shadows.

Oddly enough, I find myself—of my own free will—living in a haunted house. The place I've called home for the past twenty-seven years has a presence all its own. It makes itself known often, yet I've learned to coexist with it. And strangely, there's a certain comfort in knowing I'm never truly alone.

RONDA L. CAUDILL *is a writer, publisher, psychic medium, and owner of the haunted Nickerson Snead House in Glade Spring, Virginia. She's also the owner of Full Moon Publishing, co-owner and executive producer of Shadow Work Productions, and lead psychic medium with SRS Paranormal. She starred in* Season of the Witch, *produced by Sword & Stone Entertainment and T. Lee Films, in 2022. Ronda has written eleven books, all dealing with the paranormal and fantasy. She has co-authored four books, has had work published in several anthologies, and illustrated two books.*

No. FOURTEEN
THE NIGHT MARCHERS
KNOXVILLE, TENNESSEE

Anna Wooliver Phillips

It was three a.m., the witching hour. I could not sleep. I'd had minor surgery that week, and in misery roamed the kitchen seeking cold water and a way to pass the night. It was late August, incredibly hot, and the moon was full. The summer night was bright, and I could hear the cacophony of night bugs in the still of the darkness, even in my kitchen. As I looked through the window into the garden at my eerily illuminated and desiccated corn stalks, the noises of the night stopped.

The atmosphere in the kitchen suddenly felt like a vacuum. It was intensely silent. It felt cold and heavy. In the distance I heard something familiar getting steadily louder. Drumming. The rhythmic thudding reminded me of a timpani, a deep, repetitive, staccato resonance that was quickly approaching.

Answers ran rapid fire across my consciousness as my rational brain tried to identify what was happening.

A midweek party at three a.m.?

A passing car with the stereo on blast?

I realized I was extremely alert. The hair on my forearms rose as my hackles registered that this was something *very* different. It sounded like people approaching, walking toward and then by my house. I could hear them from the *inside*.

I heard twigs breaking.
Footfalls.
Drums.
It sounded like people walking through a thick wood, not my modern-day lawn. I was frozen in place, staring into the dark night. Our security lights stayed off, and in the darkness I detected no movement. The sounds of drumming gradually faded.
My ears popped. I jumped.
The kitchen was fine. The crickets were back. A cicada screamed. Just another hot Tennessee night.

Nobody was going to believe this one, and like most spooky things I encounter, I kept it to myself.
Was it a time slip?
An echo?
I don't understand why or how, but I felt fairly certain I knew where the marchers were heading. It was the right time of year and close to the correct time of day. My night marchers were likely heading to a massacre.

Nestled in my urban, mid-century modern neighborhood is a cemetery that marks the spot of an eighteenth century pioneer massacre at a frontier cabin known as Cavett's Station.

On September 25, 1793, three men and ten women and children were in the path of a war party heading to attack the frontier settlement of Knoxville. A thousand Chickamauga Cherokee and Creek warriors marched over a ridge near dawn, saw the smoke from Alexander Cavett's fortified blockhouse cabin and attacked. Thirteen men, women, and children were slain. The message the warriors left to the other settlers on their lands was clear.

Neighbors arrived to a scene of horror: a burned cabin, slaughtered livestock, and mutilated corpses. They buried the dead in a mass grave.

Today the spot is softer, and lower than the earth around the other burials. A monument honors those who died that day, slaking the war party's anger with their horrific deaths and saving the frontier town of Knoxville. I heard an army of night marchers, retracing their journey toward a lone cabin in the woods just before dawn.

ANNA WOOLIVER PHILLIPS *is a native of Knoxville, Tennessee and is a University of Tennessee alumna. She's usually in her urban garden when not moonlighting as a local librarian and small business owner. Momma to a bitty baby, a black cat, and a standard poodle, Anna takes her husband to cemeteries and graveyards around the world and writes non-fiction and fiction inspired by her Appalachian heritage. Her story* The House on Bluebird Drive *appeared in* 24 Tales: More Appalachian Ghost Stories, Legends & Mysteries.

FIFTEEN
THE LEGEND OF DISMAL BLUFF

ANDERSON COUNTY, TENNESSEE

Joshua Anderson

Here in East Tennessee, we are surrounded by place names that no longer have any connection to their grim origin. Ball Camp is named for a long hunter who ignored repeated warnings to leave and was killed by the Cherokee. Boyd's Creek is named for a trapper whose skinned body was stretched out on a boulder in the stream, serving as a warning to others. Some places rebound and thrive like nothing bad ever happened. Others are cursed. Dismal Bluff, just north of Knoxville in Anderson County where Dismal Creek runs through Wolf Valley, in Chestnut Ridge's shadow, is cursed.

Before this community ever dotted a surveyor's map, it was part of a vast Native American hunting ground used by the Cherokee and Creeks. They traveled through it along a river they called the Pellissippi. We call it the Clinch. By the 1790s, the Cherokee were divided over the terms of the Treaty of the Holston. The loss of ancestral lands, and the failure of the United States government to uphold its treaty obligations preventing the encroachment of white settlers onto what land remained motivated a large faction of Cherokee to hostility. Knoxville itself was under constant threat of attack. So, twenty miles into the wilderness was far too dangerous for pioneers to venture. Unless, of course, they were sociopaths. Then it was the perfect place to hide.

Joshua Harper and William Harper were North Carolina Scotsmen who found themselves pushing farther and farther westward to outrun the law. Some historians claim they were brothers. Others claim they were cousins. What we know for certain is that they were sons of bitches. Unlike some of their contemporaries who looked west for a fresh start to escape their past, the Harpes preferred the frontier for the unfettered access it gave them to rape, murder, and pillage.

During the American Revolution, the pair sided with the British Crown––a seemingly safe bet. As loyalists, they're described in T. Marshall Smith's *Legends of the War of Independence, and of the Earlier Settlements in the West,* as being part of paramilitary rape gangs that savaged the Carolina countryside during the war. Like many Tories after the war, they fled. Shortening their surname from Harper to Harpe, Joshua began going by Micajah, or "Big Harpe" and the diminutive William came to be known as Willy or "Little Harpe." They continued to migrate west and, for a time, lived among the Cherokee and Chickamauga. The Cherokee had also been allies of the British and loyalists, which is likely how the Harpes established their connection.

By the time the Harpes got to Knoxville in the mid-1790s, their skills at torture and mutilation were well-honed. Not long after arriving they brutally murdered a man by the name of Johnson through disembowelment. After filling his body cavity with rocks, and urinating on the corpse for good measure, they dumped their victim in the Tennessee River. It was the first recorded instance of what would become their trademark method of slaughter and evidence disposal. The Harpes were already social pariahs in town because of suspicions of livestock theft, but after the murder of Mr. Johnson, staying in Knoxville was no longer an option.

Leaving wasn't a much better alternative. Large numbers of disillusioned Cherokee were in the countryside. Gambling on their knowledge of Cherokee customs and language, and the hope that territorial governor and militia commander John Sevier wouldn't bother chasing them, they slipped out of town and into the woods.

They took a woman named Rebecca with them. She didn't care much for Big Harpe, but she despised Little Harpe. They fought constantly, much to the ire of Big Harpe, who was not known for patience. His motives for slashing a throat were as trivial as a snoring roommate. His victims: anyone who inconvenienced him. Native and foreign. Free and enslaved. Men, women, and children. Even his own children. According to R. E. Banta's book *The Ohio,* the killing of his own infant child was the only murder Big Harpe ever expressed contrition over.

The trio settled in the area we now call Dismal Bluff and built a small cabin about a mile from the portion of the river called Eagle Bend. There was a ford at the bend, and a Cherokee encampment on the opposite bank. Attempts were made to scare the Harpes away, but at over six feet, and always armed with a rifle, tomahawk, and knife (the knife being his instrument of choice), Big Harpe didn't scare worth a damn. Then one day, some warriors crossed the river and found Rebecca alone in the cabin. The Harpes returned home to an empty cabin and an obvious struggle. They found Rebecca's mutilated body hanging in a tree overlooking the Dismal Bluff.

Enraged, but not foolhearted, the Harpes slipped across Eagle Ford and waited all night until the men of the encampment headed out for the salt springs near present-day Oliver Springs. It was far enough away that the Harpes could take their time. They methodically butchered every woman and child in the camp until being interrupted by something Big Harpe hadn't counted on: a small band of warriors returning from a hunt.

Local legend has it that Little Harpe was mortally wounded in the ensuing battle, and Big Harpe fled farther north to Kentucky, where he continued his killing spree. Little Harpe barely made it back to the cabin. As he lay dying, Rebecca, who according to lore had transformed into a witch upon her death, had taunted him. He died in the cabin. With nobody left to bury him, his bones remained in the dilapidated structure until another settler came along and claimed the homestead.

Even after the land was reclaimed, his bones were still not buried but instead stored in the attic as a curiosity, perhaps contributing to his spirit's restlessness. In any case, from the time of his and Rebecca's gruesome deaths, the bluff was never the same. Cabin fires, and later, house fires, would plague the area for two more centuries. Even a devastating flood of Wolf Valley in 1937 was blamed on the duel between The Ghost of Wolf Valley and The Witch of Dismal Bluff, according to a *Clinton Courier* newspaper article published in 1971.

The legend has largely passed from living memory, but the location still has an eerie, cursed feel to it. The highest elevation in the valley, the Chestnut Ridge Landfill, burns the excess underground methane off, with a flame shooting several yards into the sky, visible every night from the interstate. When the wind blows just right, the blaze is accompanied by the stench of sulfur.

When the 21st century finally arrived and the rural route box numbers gave way to more streamlined mailing addresses, the name of Dismal Bluff was changed to Mountain View. Perhaps that was a conspiracy by local realtors to give the place a more marketable name.

According to Schram and Tibbetts' *Introduction to Criminology: Why They Do It*, the Harpes are widely regarded as America's first serial killers. Scholars attribute anywhere from thirty-nine to fifty murders to Big Harpe and Little Harpe. While the local legend maintains Little Harpe met his end in Wolf Valley, documented contemporary accounts say a vigilante posse caught up with him on the Natchez Trace and hanged him. There's even physical evidence for this version.

The Harpe's trackers, in their zealous pursuit of justice, didn't think hanging Little Harpe was enough. They took turns cutting off Little Harpe's fingers and toes and distributing the amputated trophies as souvenirs. Several were passed down through the generations as family heirlooms. Some have ended up donated to the state archives over the years, presumably by people who would've preferred inheriting Pappaw's pocket watch instead of a mummified toe.

Regardless of which version of Little Harpe's demise you believe, Big Harpe lived to kill another day. His infamy extends beyond the Legend of Dismal Bluff and the Natchez Trace. He finally met his match up in Kentucky, when an avenging husband and father cut his head off and left it on a pike along the road outside his home. An 1840 publication called *The United States Criminal Calendar*, references the incident and that the road would come to be known as Harpe's Head Road. Another gruesome namesake tied to a memory time forgot.

JOSHUA ANDERSON *is a ninth-generation East Tennessean with a deep love of the region's history and culture. A graduate of the University of Tennessee with a degree in agriculture, he operates his family's Century Farm in Clinton. He is serving his second term as an Anderson County Commissioner and chairs the Anderson County Library Board. He also serves on the advisory board of the Norris Area Community Foundation and has been an actor with Norris Little Theatre.*

SIXTEEN
A MARK THAT STANDS THE TEST OF TIME

JIM THORPE, PENNSYLVANIA

Thom Tracy

Leading up to his execution, Alec Campbell could hear and feel the hammering of nails as a scaffold was being built inside the Carbon County Jail, right next to his cell. Undertakers had already visited Campbell and three others to measure them for caskets. His wife and two sisters had to pass the gallows before reaching his cell to bid him farewell.

Executions in Pennsylvania hadn't been staged publicly since 1834, which didn't stop some prominent mine and railroad owners. At their behest, a new high sheriff had whipped up a circus atmosphere in this small eastern Pennsylvania town then known as Mauch Chunk. His first act was to open the jail doors to the public. Hundreds of onlookers rushed in and gawked at the condemned men. Reporters swarmed their cells and children danced up and down on the trapdoor that would drop beneath the feet of the four men who would soon hang simultaneously and side by side.

On the morning of June 21, 1877, shackled and headed to his doom, Campbell scooped up a handful of black dust and slapped the wall of his cell.

"There is the proof of my words," he said. "That mark of mine will never be wiped out. There it will remain forever to shame a county that hanged an innocent man."

It was a sad end to a story that once held so much promise.

Campbell had prospered since immigrating from County Donegal, Ireland, to the United States eleven years earlier. After settling in Pennsylvania and finding work as a miner, he saved enough money to buy a hotel and tavern in the town of Lansford. Perhaps unfairly, stories circulated about bodies buried in the basement of that hotel known as the Columbia House.

In addition to becoming a successful businessman, he rose to division chief of the Ancient Order of Hibernians, an Irish Catholic fraternal organization established decades earlier. Many thought it a front for the Molly Maguires, a secretive band that fought for miners' rights. Its roots trace back to Ireland and its spirit may have sailed across the Atlantic with Campbell and boatloads of his countrymen.

Some things hadn't changed. In the old country, Irish peasants fought Welsh and English landlords for the means to survive. The same held true in the Keystone State's coalfields, where mostly Irish miners clashed with English or Welsh bosses. The dispute was simple: Working conditions and wages were horrible, and the owners did nothing to improve them, leading to conflict ranging from work stoppages to attempts at organization. Even murder.

To maintain order, mine owners established their very own Coal and Iron Police, which had been granted jurisdictional standing. In fact, when Alec Campbell was tried the Commonwealth simply supplied the courtroom—and the gallows.

After a Welsh mining boss was shot dead while walking to work in Tamaqua, three men were accused of the crime. Campbell wasn't charged. Initially. An indictment was handed down after an Irishman with the Pinkerton Detective Agency uncovered anecdotal evidence that Campbell arranged the murder of the mining boss, who once refused to employ him. That snub provided motive for the prosecution, and the Hibernian was arrested.

A hanging judge from outside Carbon County was brought in to preside over the murder trial. The jury of his "peers" was composed of Welsh and German immigrants, four of whom did not speak English. Not a single juror shared Campbell's faith or nationality. In this case, as in so many others, Irish need not apply.

The key witness offered testimony in exchange for a deal that spared his own neck from the noose. Law enforcement knew the informant had committed crimes, including murder. He'd admitted as much.

The circle of rope tightened.

In his book, *A Molly Maguire Story*, Patrick Campbell (Alec's great nephew) identified inconsistencies in witness accounts but defense arguments fell flat or objections were never sustained. Campbell was found guilty as an accessory to murder before the fact. Appeals failed and a stay of execution from the governor did not arrive.

Campbell's heart would not surrender without a fight on that summer morning. It beat for fifteen minutes after the hatch dropped and the rope did its job.

And the mark he left on the wall?

Despite attempts to paint over or scrub it away, his final declaration endures. Alec's great-grandnephew, Attorney J. Brian Campbell, in a recent visit to the Carbon County Jail Museum, asked an attendant about it.

"I am not a religious man," the guide said. "But I swear to you the handprint comes through the wall all the way to the other side."

On which side of justice, it's eternally tough to tell.

THOM TRACY *is the author of* The Kings of Cork Lane, *a memoir about family and friends written through a baseball lens. He's had stories in* "23 Tales: Appalachian Ghost Stories, Legends & Other Mysteries" *and* "24 Tales: More Appalachian Ghost Stories Legends & Mysteries." *He lives in West Pittston, Pennsylvania, and enjoys bicycling and collecting pre-war baseball cards.*

SEVENTEEN
SPIRITS OF OLD GRAY

KNOXVILLE, TENNESSEE

Laura Still

One block south of the historic Old North Knoxville neighborhood, bordered by Broadway on the east and Cooper Street on the west, is the first cemetery in Knoxville. The gates of Old Gray are wrought iron flanked by engraved stone pillars, and stand open during the day, welcoming neighborhood strollers and visitors to enjoy a peaceful green oasis tucked into the busy urban streets. At sunset the portals wing shut, allowing the 14-acre property to sleep securely through the night, but anyone familiar with Old Gray will tell you that not all the inhabitants rest easy.

I had heard some of these stories when I began the research for *A Haunted History of Knoxville* in 2013 and knew I had to include a chapter on the spirits of Old Gray. That started my association with the cemetery board of trustees. After the book came out, the executive director asked me how she could keep me coming to see her, and I offered to start doing guided tours as an additional fundraiser to their yearly fall reenactment event. My love affair with the hidden history of Old Gray officially began.

With over 9,000 burials, I know it will take more than my lifetime to find all the stories, but that's a great problem to have. Since the big annual event—now called Spirits of Old Gray—happens in the fall, they request a tour full of ghosts, murder, and various types of mayhem. Though there is no shortage of material, my favorites to share are the stories of women who were often victims of violence from those who professed to love them most.

Martin Woody and Annie Lowe

Martin Woody was a respected businessman and brick mason in Knoxville in the 1870s, and the papers frequently mentioned his involvement in the construction of commercial and residential buildings. He oversaw the brickwork on the Third Presbyterian Church, the palatial homes of Col. C. M. McGhee, James Cowan, and other wealthy clients, and served on the Board of Alderman under Mayor Peter Staub in 1875. He had a reputation for skilled workmanship and as a hardworking, civic-minded family man, but in hindsight the darker sides to his character appear.

Mary W. Crush, a relation of his wife, moved into the Woody home as an orphaned child. In 1872, at the age of twelve or thirteen, she sued Martin Woody, and the judge appointed a new guardian for her. The dispute appears to involve some land Martin Woody held in trust for young Mary, but he must have been doing something particularly shady, for the judge also ordered that the new guardian sell the land on Mary's behalf and that it must be valued at no less than $300. In those days a verdict for a preteen against a successful businessman, also her guardian, was almost unheard of—one can't help but wonder what sort of bad behavior of Martin's moved the judge to rule in Mary's favor.

Still, Martin Woody's reputation as a skilled and reliable contractor survived, and he was busier than ever in 1879, working on the homes of his upscale clientele and downtown businesses: law offices on Clinch and the brickwork for the Hattie House hotel, where the Farragut building stands today. But before the end of that year, Martin ended both his good name and his life by his treatment of another woman.

Her name was Annie Lowe. Described "a young woman of attractive appearance," she moved from her birthplace in Coal Creek to Knoxville sometime around 1877, seeking work as a seamstress. As often happened in those days, the naive young girl from the country was lured into prostitution. Martin Woody, that fine upstanding businessman, was one of her frequent customers. It was said that he became obsessed with Annie, and she fled the city, perhaps to escape his attentions, but she returned to Knoxville in 1879, and tried to start over.

Annie took a room in a respectable house in South Knoxville, at a time when there was no vehicle or pedestrian bridge over the river—the 1870 bridge at the end of Gay Street had blown down in a storm, and had not yet been replaced. A railroad bridge, called the Maryville bridge, could be traversed by walking on the tracks or illegally borrowing the handcart. Most people, if they crossed at all, went by boat on the "lower ferry" manned by a riverman named Alex Doyle. It seems Annie wanted to make it hard for any of her former acquaintances to find her.

But it wasn't enough to stop Martin Woody. He crossed the river on Tuesday night, August 26, 1879, and found Annie at her rooming house. She asked him to leave, he refused, and they argued fiercely before Annie retreated into her room, threatening to shoot Woody if he didn't leave her alone. He forced his way in as she retrieved a gun from her trunk, and they began to struggle. Annie said later she didn't know if she fired the gun or it went off in the scuffle. Either way, Martin Woody was shot in the stomach and died before the doctor arrived thirty minutes later. Annie related her story to the physician, a Dr. Deaderick, who left her alone in her room while he questioned the landlord and family about what they had heard and sent for the police.

Before they could arrive, Annie Lowe, in despair over her predicament, put the gun to her own chest. The doctor rushed back to her on hearing the shot, but though she lingered in terrible pain for several hours, he could not save her. Poor Annie—she knew too well the world would take the side of the successful businessman over a ruined woman and chose to shoot herself rather than hang for murder.

A reporter noted that Annie's sister had come to claim her body, and said she was buried "at Ebenezer." It doesn't say "cemetery" in the paper; however there was an Ebenezer Cemetery on the site of the original Cedar Springs Cemetery. I found no listing of her marker in records, but that burial ground contains several unmarked graves. The sister told the reporter that Annie had a deceased child there and she planned to bury Annie alongside. Visitors to that old cemetery have long told the tale of the evening breeze carrying the sound of a soft voice singing a lullaby—Annie, lost no more, singing to her baby.

Martin Woody, in spite of his disgraceful death, was eulogized by the Knoxville papers and buried at Old Gray with a fine marble tombstone in the Crush plot with his wife's family. Twenty years later Martin's wife was buried next to him with a matching stone, still nicely preserved. But Martin's stone cracked straight across, twice, before being completely destroyed. Whether by vandals or the unforgiving spirits of his in-laws, it's hard to say.

Rebecca Eckle and Yell

Not far away from the Crush family plot, cemetery visitors tell of another voice sometimes crooning a lullaby but breaking into deep sobs of a grief too deep for words. This is said to be the spirit of Rebecca Eckle, a mother struck down by the person she loved most.

Rebecca Eckle was the wife of William Eckle, a "well-respected member of the city," according to the April 20, 1880, editions of the Knoxville papers. She was the mother of an adult son named Yelverton "Yell" Eckle and grandmother to his two children. William and Rebecca were members of Church Street Methodist Church when it was still part of the Methodist Episcopal denomination.

Yell Eckle had a reputation as a belligerent drunkard who often came home inebriated and angry, and would fight with his wife, raising a considerable disturbance. His parents lived next door and when Rebecca heard her son shouting, she would go to the house to try to calm him down and protect his wife and children.

On the evening in question, Rebecca heard her son roaring at his family on the porch of his house, and ran next door to reason with him. The presence of his mother was usually enough to calm Yell, and her daughter-in-law took the opportunity to slip over to the fence and ask a neighbor to take the baby out of harm's way. While she was gone, Yell picked up a slat from the baby's cradle and struck his mother in the back of the head. Rebecca fell, striking her skull on the porch floor.

This was witnessed by a servant girl across the street. A neighbor standing with the servant ran instantly to help Rebecca but found her already dead. Yell sat down on the step, crying, and the neighbor told him he had killed his mother. Witnesses heard Yell reply that he would kill every one of them. Policeman Mose Smith then arrived and took Yell into custody.

Later at the jail when Yell sobered up, he remembered nothing of the tragedy, and had to be shown his mother's body before he would believe she was dead. Confronted with it, he said only "Did I do that?" and began weeping. He was convicted of manslaughter a few months later, and none of his family attended the trial. He died in a tuberculosis ward in St. Louis in 1901.

William Eckle purchased a fine tombstone for his wife, Rebecca, and the funeral was well-attended, as was the burial at Old Gray. Her stone is still standing, somewhat weathered but still legible after all these years. It is in a style that has a stone-bordered bed of earth at the front of the stone, with the idea that flowers or small shrubs can be planted there to honor the deceased. But for a lady who met her death by a blow with a piece of her grandchild's crib, it's a little creepy that her husband chose this style: it's called a cradle grave.

LAURA STILL *is a poet, playwright, and author. She created Knoxville Walking Tours in 2012 and works full-time as a storyteller and walking history guide. She has researched and written fifteen tours, including three ghost walks. She partners with the Knoxville History Project and proceeds from her tours support it and other history-oriented Knoxville nonprofits. Co-owner of Celtic Cat Publishing since 2016, she has written four books:* Guardians (2009), Acts of the Apostles, Vol. 1, (2010), A Haunted History of Knoxville (2014), *and* A Fair Shake: The Leaders of the Fight for Women's Rights in Knoxville (2021).

Eighteen
THE SHY MADAM
KEYSER, WEST VIRGINIA

Allison Churchill

I don't know if there was a time I didn't believe in ghosts or didn't love getting spooked, from *Ghostbusters* to Michael Jackson's *Thriller* video to the Halloween episodes of *Unsolved Mysteries* and Nickelodeon's *Are You Afraid of the Dark*? I checked out every ghost story collection in my school's library. I learned all the signs that something from another plane was nearby: electronics turning on and off; the room suddenly turning cold; animals growling at thin air. And today, when something a little weird happens, I just presume a ghost is saying "hi" and hope it's a nice one.

That's how I knew that my first full-time job, at the *Mineral Daily News-Tribune* in Keyser, West Virginia, was a good fit. Some people know they've taken the right job when they meet their colleagues or they hear about the projects they'll get to do. For me, it was finding out the office was haunted.

It all began at the turn of the 20th century, when Keyser bustled with industry. Three railroad companies, woolen mills, and coal mines brought workers to the town. Mother McGann was there to help the men spend their money, running a brothel upstairs from a downtown saloon. Decades later, the same building hosted the *News-Tribune*. I arrived in February 2002 and the male employees' eyes twinkled any time they declared they were open to being haunted by Mother McGann. By then, Keyser wasn't booming anymore. The closest mall and movie theater were 20 miles away in Cumberland, Maryland. I didn't mind working in the evenings since there wasn't much to do (I also enjoyed getting to sleep in). Not that the newsroom itself was great. Due to a lack of windows it was always dim; it was also stale, since there wasn't a direct path from either door to let in fresh air.

My first few months passed without any visits from Mother McGann, though I gave her plenty of opportunities. Some newspapers spread jobs like page design and photography around to several employees, but in addition to reporting and writing, I managed the lifestyles section and occasionally the front section. Many nights found me in the newsroom after the other reporters had gone home, trying to make a headline fit or fact-checking a story.

At one point I was able to go straight to Mother McGann's stomping grounds. A few employees realized our schedules had aligned, and we could take advantage of happy hour at the cantina across the street from the paper together. Before we went our separate ways that night, Brenda, who lived in one of the apartments above the front office, asked if anyone needed to use her bathroom. The apartments were where the brothel was! Surely there would be an extra set of footsteps, some creaks in the floor where no humans were standing. Maybe a waft of old-timey perfume or stale beer.

Alas, I got up and down the stairs without incident, despite walking as slowly as possible.

But then, the flash. It was during the summer, a late afternoon. The front office was still open and busy. Three of us were in the newsroom. Two of us saw it. A silent muzzle flash, just a couple of feet below the ceiling. I caught the eye of our sports reporter,

Brian, and raised an eyebrow. From his desk diagonal to mine, he raised one back. Our general reporter, Jon, was on the phone and oblivious, despite being directly across from Brian. And it was a small newsroom–the guys' desks couldn't have been more than three feet apart. None of the lightbulbs that kept the newsroom yellow were out. No one had a camera out.

The next day, Brian and I found ourselves in the front office talking to one of the receptionists. After a minute or so, she excused herself to take a phone call. We took the opportunity to again raise an eyebrow at each other.

"You saw that yesterday, right?" he asked.

"Yep."

"Do you know what it was?"

"Nope."

"Do you think it was…" he asked, as we both looked up toward the ceiling.

"Maybe."

That autumn, having realized there wasn't any room for advancement for me at the *News-Tribune,* and that I needed to shake things up in my personal life, I decided to apply to grad schools and move home at the end of the year to save money. The internet service at the office was more stable than in my apartment, so a few nights a week I'd stay after sending the lifestyles section off to the press.

One October night I glanced over at our managing editor's desk and saw the chair turning. Hmmm. Tony, the managing editor, had not been in for several hours and no one else had been in the newsroom. Or any of the rooms, for that matter. I hadn't heard anyone from the printing press building come in the side door to clock in. And if someone had come in, and been followed by a gust of wind strong enough to blow down the hall, make two lefts and move a chair, that wind would have also been strong enough to make paper fly off my desk!

That seemed to be a good sign that it was time to go home and bid Mother McGann a good night. Not that I was afraid of her, of course. I just didn't think I'd be all that productive with a visitor.

ALLISON CHURCHILL *grew up in Pennsylvania and now lives in the Bronx, but she comes from a family with deep roots in wild and wonderful West Virginia. Allison did make it to graduate school after a very unplanned turn as an Army public affairs specialist. She has written for Scholastic's* DynaMath *and* MATH, Guideposts, Reserve + National Guard, *and* Military Families *magazines. She currently works as a digital content editor for the New York City Department of Health and Mental Hygiene.*

NINETEEN
The End of the Line: Brushy Mountain State Penitentiary

Petros, Tennessee

Matthew Sorge

As a paranormal researcher and medium, I've traveled across America searching for truth, chasing mysteries, and witnessing the unexplainable at countless haunted locations. Some sites give you pause, others strike fear in your heart, while still others invoke a deep sadness. In the mountains of East Tennessee, Brushy Mountain State Penitentiary embodies all three in equal measure. Opened in 1896 and operated by the Tennessee Department of Corrections until it closed in 2009, the maximum-security facility earned its nickname as "the end of the line." Brushy housed the worst of the worst—murderers, gang leaders, and violent offenders with average sentences exceeding 200 years.

I've investigated Brushy four times. My first visit was in 2019, and that night is etched in my memory. Surrounded by sheer rock walls and treacherous terrain, Brushy's location is as unforgiving as its reputation. Driving up the long, twisting road toward the prison, I felt energy fill the night air like the calm before a summer storm.

Completed in the mid-1930s, the stone prison was intentionally designed in the shape of a Greek cross, symbolizing hope for inmate reform. But reform was nowhere to be found.

Though meant to hold 676 inmates, Brushy regularly housed more than 900. Overcrowding plagued the prison for decades. Corruption was rampant. Guards stole from prisoners and from the state. Some aided in revenge killings. Others turned a blind eye. Disease was just as deadly as the violence. Tuberculosis, pneumonia, and typhoid fever swept through the prison regularly.

Yet the moment Brushy came into view, a strangely comforting anxiety knotted my stomach. The building is imposing, with an almost magnetic pull: a mix of anticipation and nervousness, like riding a roller coaster for the first time.

The entranceway felt flat, buffered from the rest of the structure. That feeling changed when we passed into the cell block and a heavy sadness engulfed me.

Our team passed through a large steel door and entered the auditorium. Al James, who was ahead of me, suddenly stopped dead in his tracks. This was still early in Al's paranormal career, and his reaction was completely out of character. Normally, he would rush into the most sinister of locations, ready to face anything. This time, he was still. I also felt the cold, heavy, oppressive force. We both hesitated.

This area, for me, would prove to be the most unsettling part of the entire prison. We explored for a while, trying to get a feel for the room. I noticed Ronda Caudill, our lead medium, humming a classical-sounding tune and moving her hands as though conducting an invisible orchestra.

"What are you doing?" I asked.

"What do you mean?" she answered.

I explained what I had witnessed.

"Well, I see this man," she said. "He's dressed nicely, and he's humming this music. He seems completely unaware of the prison he's in."

We paused, conducting an EVP (Electronic Voice Phenomena) session in hopes of capturing a ghostly voice or perhaps the conductor's melody. After several minutes and no otherworldly responses, we moved on to the chapel.

That's when I sensed a male energy, first lurking ahead–and then creeping behind us. I was a few feet behind my teammates when I heard a man's voice yell, "Hello." I quickly turned around, shining my flashlight down the dark hallway behind me.

It was empty.

We made our way down to the hole—the solitary confinement cells beneath the chapel. It felt almost too cliché, a slice of hell hidden beneath a place of worship. The hallway was dark, tight, and oppressive. The thick steel doors of the cells were cold and damp, with only a tiny slit allowing a sliver of light to penetrate, even during the day. I felt trapped.

I'm a career firefighter. Dark, tight spaces don't usually faze me, but I needed air. So I retreated upstairs to regain my composure. Looking up at the window, I saw, for the second time in my paranormal career, a full-body apparition standing and staring back at me. The figure was in the middle window, behind a locked door inaccessible to visitors. We were the only people on the site, yet there it stood.

I stood transfixed, then the figure disappeared. My heart raced as I rejoined the team. Teammate Wes Spurgeon, Al, and I returned to the hole, determined to make contact with the dark figure. The temperature had dropped further, and the weight of despair seemed heavier. We decided to use a spirit box for real-time communication.

I positioned myself in the doorway of a cell, my back to the cell as I filmed the session. My frame barely fit, but suddenly I was shoved from behind.

Cold fingers gripped the back of my neck, pushing me away

from the door. Stunned, I commanded, "You are not welcome to harm us!"

Nothing happened for several more minutes, so we regrouped in the cafeteria, the site of many violent attacks and deaths. Others exploring this part of the prison have heard footsteps, seen shadowy figures, and dodged chairs that had been thrown through the air.

Ronda and I decided to turn off every flashlight and sit in complete darkness. The moment the lights went out, the room came alive. We could feel movement around us on all sides. The ambient moonlight cast eerie shadows across the room, and we caught glimpses of a human-like figure just outside the cafeteria entrance. Suddenly, we heard movement in the kitchen behind us and the sound of a cell door slamming down the hall.

Then, as quickly as it started, the energy lifted. An eerie silence fell over the prison, and the rest of the investigation was quiet.

Life at Brushy was brutal from the beginning. Its original structure was a four-story wooden stockade that housed 210 prisoners, all sentenced to hard labor in the newly established Frozen Head Mine. The work was back-breaking, and inmates were expected to meet daily quotas of coal. Those who failed were beaten in the yard with a seven-foot leather strap. Many were killed by the conditions. Others were murdered. Violence was an everyday occurrence. The mines themselves were deadly. The region's unstable geology created methane pockets and collapses. Fires and explosions were constant threats. There were no safety standards. Inmates were disposable labor.

In 1932, former inmate Rex Cosby risked his life to expose the horrors. Serving fifteen months for forgery, he wrote a series of articles detailing the conditions, using his real name and fully aware of the danger that posed. During his sentence, he saw thirteen men die. Another former inmate, a World War I veteran, said he would rather face the trenches of Europe than return to the mines of Brushy.

These testimonies ignited public outrage. Political leaders, clergy, and local citizens demanded change. The state responded by constructing the stone fortress that stands to this day.

Mining continued, along with several violent revolts. Prisoners repeatedly took guards hostage in protest of the conditions. After several inmates serving time for petty crimes died in yet another mine collapse, the state finally shut down mining operations in 1966. The last load of coal pulled from Frozen Head Mine marked the end of an era of forced labor.

Violence remained until the end. One inmate was hacked to death with a meat cleaver in the kitchen. Another was killed when a hammer was driven into his skull in the cafeteria line. Guards were sometimes outnumbered thirty to one. Brushy finally shut down in 2009. The costs were too high, the buildings too old, the staff too thin.

Each of my subsequent visits to Brushy Mountain has been just as unique and hair-raising. On one moonlit night, we encountered the spirit of Joe, an inmate who was murdered while lighting a cigarette. His throat was slit from behind, and he died in seconds—never having the chance to light his smoke. Investigators often light a cigarette for Joe, and many teams have documented the ghostly moment when the lit cigarette glows brighter, as if someone is taking a drag. We tried this too, and to our amazement, the cigarette grew brighter as the meter spiked. We continued to speak with Joe, and again, the meter spiked, followed by the cherry of the cigarette glowing brighter. We asked him to take a drag, and on command, the meter spiked once more, the cigarette glowing brightly.

Then, just as suddenly as the encounter began, it ended.

The otherworldly experiences I've had at Brushy Mountain are too many to recount in one sitting. It is a place with a violent, bloody past responsible for over 10,000 deaths in its 113 years of operation. It's no surprise it remains a paranormal hotbed as the restless souls of countless inmates continue serving their sentences long into the afterlife, condemned to relive the hell they once called home.

Today, Brushy Mountain lives on as a distillery, concert venue, and tourist destination. Visitors can explore the haunted halls, hear the stories, and even take paranormal and historical tours. Even if you don't believe in ghosts, Brushy remains a dark chapter in the history of American incarceration—a monument to pain, cruelty, and survival.

It truly was the end of the line.

———

MATTHEW SORGE *has been a career firefighter for over two decades. After an unexplained encounter, he began his quest for answers to the unknown and unexplained. Over the years, hundreds of investigations at some of America's most infamous hauntings and countless residential cases have taught him that paranormal phenomena not only exist but have an impact on those who encounter it. His story,* A Shadow in the Attic of Deery Inn *appeared in* 23 Tales: Appalachian Ghost Stories, Legends & Other Mysteries. *Learn more about Matthew and his work at www.srsparanormal.com.*

TWENTY
UNCLE LEON AND UNCLE ERNIE

KNOXVILLE, TENNESSEE

Sharon Larisey

When my two cousins and I were little kids in Knoxville, Tennessee, our grandmother, Ouida Larisey, would sit us down in her dark apartment and pull out her scrapbooks. The three of us would listen, wide-eyed, as she theatrically told us about her family. What follows is a story she told us about something that happened to her brother while he was stationed in France during World War I.

Ernie and his Uncle Leon were very, very close. Leon had been sort of a second, very much-loved father to Ernie when he was growing up, and they kept in touch as best they could with Ernie fighting in France and Leon living in Charleston, South Carolina. Leon had been ill, and Ernie hadn't heard from him in a while, but times being what they were, he was not very worried as he knew the family would take the best care of Leon they could. If anything happened, they would move heaven and earth to get a message to Ernie, no matter where he was.

Ernie was on night patrol in one of the small villages that dotted the French countryside when he spotted a figure standing under a lamppost about halfway down a deserted street. As he walked down the street, the figure seemed more and more familiar to him. As he drew even with the man, he realized it was Uncle Leon.

Ernie, taken a bit aback and happy to see his dear relative looking so good, said, "Uncle Leon, what are you doing here?"

The figure turned, smiled at him, then walked off down an alley between two buildings.

Ernie, still a bit in shock, paused, then ran down the alley after Leon... but Leon had disappeared. The alley was a blind one, with no access into the buildings on either side, and a solid brick wall at the end, there was nowhere for Leon to have hidden, or escaped to. More than a little confused, Ernie continued his patrol, and life for a soldier during wartime went on. A few weeks later, he got a letter from his family. His Uncle Leon had passed away in Charleston...on the night and at the time that Ernie had seen him standing under that lamppost, in a small village in France, during the first World War.

Some connections, love being one, are stronger than death.

SHARON LARISEY *is an East Tennessee girl who rambled to Chicago and then to California, where she lived in the land of Haight & Ashbury, wandered in the desert for twenty years and ended up at the beach before returning to her home mountains. She is a shutter bug, cookbook hoarder, baker babe, dedicated liberal and unapologetic batter addict... not necessarily in that order.*

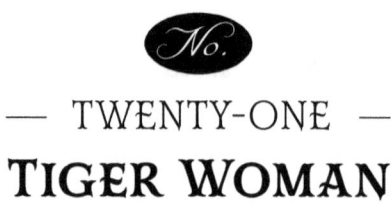

— TWENTY-ONE —
TIGER WOMAN

LETCHER COUNTY, KENTUCKY

Sheree Combs

My brother, Mike, three neighbor kids, and I headed up the path that curved past the old barn, not far from our home on Blair Branch, in Letcher County, Kentucky. We stopped halfway up the mountain to climb a boulder, daring each other to jump off before continuing on. A covey of contented, scab-kneed kids on an adventure in the woods until someone whispered, "Wait, I think I heard something."

We grew quiet and motionless as statues, the caws of birds and murmur of insects the only sounds as we strained our ears to listen. At the sound of a rustle in the decayed leaves and tree branches our eyes widened and faces paled until our freckles stood ready to jump and run for it. We held our collective breaths until my brother shouted, "It's the *Tiger Woman!*"

Then it was each girl or boy for himself as we scrambled through the thickets and briers, screaming at the top of our lungs all the way down the mountain. Our legs quivered in relief once we reached level ground, hot-faced, gasping for air, hearts frantic as bird wings in our chests, arms and legs scratched and bloody. The dank odor of ancient woods and a sweaty sheen of fear coated us like an extra layer of skin.

I dared not glance back once we surged full throttle down the mountain. With the image of an upright cat-creature with glowing eyes pulsing in my brain, the thought of seeing her in hot pursuit was more than a nine-year-old girl could bear.

We grew up in a holler in the coalfields of Southeastern Kentucky with this creature who prowled the same hills we did, part woman and part tiger. Sometimes we forgot about her, but every few months her piercing, desolate screams interrupted the quiet of an afternoon or evening, reminding us of her existence. Each time she cried out, the hair on the nape of our necks rose, and our hearts beat out an ages-old terror. Her wails echoed through the mountaintops for only a minute or so, but preyed on our minds for a long time afterwards. We had no reason to question the Tiger Woman's existence. Our mother had filled our heads with eerie tales from the time we learned to talk.

"Mom, tell us scary stories. Please!"

"Okay, but I don't wanna hear you're too scared to go to sleep tonight."

In our weathered board and batten home, I slept near my younger brother and sister. Their presence provided comfort in the midst of the fright generated by those stories.

Not once did we stop to ponder how a tiger made its way to our holler–a four-mile stretch of one-lane road snaking between mountains–and became able to mate with a woman. Woven into the fabric of our lives as deeply as the sun coming up over the hills, we existed with her in wary companionship. Folks talked of her like one might speak of a neighbor, albeit one they feared or at least deeply respected.

She was as real to us as anyone we knew, but as I grew older I realized the Tiger Woman was a Blair Branch phenomenon--

other folks I met in Letcher County hadn't heard of her. Perhaps she'd followed Papaw Obie from Bell County in 1927 when he moved for work in the coal mines. Based on bone-chilling tales that came out of Steward Holler, where he was raised, she would've fit right in. Both the headless hitchhiker who jumped on the back of Papaw's horse on nights he drank too much and the ghostly musician who shoved open the cabin door, grabbed Grandpa Stewart's banjo and played all night still haunt the backwoods of my memories.

Some proclaimed the Tiger Woman a panther, a cat known for screaming like a woman being murdered. Mountain folks sometimes called them *painters*. I've listened to a panther scream in YouTube videos but couldn't detect the same sound that struck terror in our young hearts. Our Tiger Woman's cries rang out mournful and forlorn, full of suffering of the heart. If alone on the porch when she cried out, my shoulders sagged from the weight of her loneliness. I'd wonder if she wailed for the company of someone like her. This thought soon dissipated as fear got the better of me, and with my back against the wall, I edged toward the screened-door and into the safety of home.

Years later an article about the Wampus Cat led me to ponder whether this legend could be the origin of our Tiger Woman. According to lore, the Wampus Cat was once a beautiful Native American woman. The men of her tribe often went on hunting trips but the women had to stay home. This woman secretly followed her husband. She hid behind a rock, clutching the hide of a mountain cat around her, and spied on the men as they told sacred stories and performed magic. Tribal laws forbid women from listening to the stories or observing the magic. Once discovered, the men bound her into the cat skin and transformed her into a half woman half mountain cat creature, doomed to forever roam the hills alone, howling desolately in the desire to return to her normal body.

Surrounded by hills that held magic and mystery in their treetops, boulders and crevices, it wasn't a big stretch to imagine we shared our mountains with this tormented creature. The screams we heard let us know she was real. She belonged here, too. Deep in our bones we liked knowing she was out there. We sensed the fright she stirred within us brought us alive in a way we'd never be again, once we outran the innocence of childhood.

Those ancient, dark hills still hold magic for those of us who know where to look. I like to believe she's still out there, in search of redemption. Or maybe she found peace in life as the creature she became long ago. At age sixty-eight, a part of me misses her and the drama she colored my childhood in. When I drive up the holler and park where our home once stood, I stare at the mountains we shared and listen for her cry.

SHEREE STEWART COMBS *is a writer and photographer whose nonfiction has appeared in publications such as* Still: The Journal, Beyond Words Literary Magazine, Women Speak, Volume Ten, Heartwood Literary Magazine, *and* Kentucky Monthly Magazine. *Sheree lives with her husband on a small farm in Central Kentucky. She grew up in Letcher County, and travels back 'home' as much as possible. She often draws inspiration for her writing from her childhood in the mountains. Sheree enjoys gardening, walks along her road, and the Argentine Tango.*

No. TWENTY-TWO
THE HIGH RIDGE CHILD
BRISTOL, TENNESSEE

Emily Monroe

Sabrina always thought scary and weird things only happened after dark. But it was mid-afternoon when, going about her business, she carried in several bags of formula cans and baby food and placed them on the kitchen counter in the new rental house. When she came back inside with the next load she found the first bags placed neatly on the floor. Her husband John came up behind her with his own load.

"I put those on the counter," Sabrina said with a growing sense of unease.

"I'm sure they just fell off," John said. He tried not to think about it too hard since the cans would've been scattered from the fall instead of neatly sitting in the plastic grocery bags.

This wasn't the only odd occurrence.

Still, the home on Boardwalk Avenue in Bristol, Tennessee, offered a lot of extra room compared to the tiny place they had been in. The open, square downstairs layout meant two baby gates could turn the dining room into a safe play area for their three-month-old son since they could see him from the kitchen or living room. Plenty of street and driveway parking meant all six of their best friends could come over every Friday. And Steele Creek Park, 2,000 acres of wilderness, wrapped the south and west sides of the neighborhood.

It took the rest of us a while to start noticing the things Sabrina and John tried to ignore.

"Which of us left the milk out on the counter?" one of them might ask.

"What happened to the bottle I laid right here next to the sink?"

"Didn't we turn that toy off?"

With a fresh move, a young child, and each working full-time jobs, it was easier for Sabrina to let John push for logical explanations. They were first-time parents, very busy, and easily overwhelmed. They must have just forgotten.

When the toy radio that had been turned off kept loudly playing the alphabet song, John guessed he hadn't pushed the button all the way to the left. Or maybe it had an electrical short that caused it to go off randomly throughout the evening. Eventually, Sabrina discovered the toys that had "shorts" in them and caused them to go off with no one else in the room suddenly didn't have those shorts at her parents house.

In addition to that, when everyone was downstairs we could hear footsteps upstairs. Once when John and Sabrina were upstairs getting ready to go out, my boyfriend and I, waiting for them on the couch downstairs, heard someone sneeze in the kitchen.

It took little Jonathan a while to get used to the house. At first he never wanted to be on the floor, and would cry to be picked up again. He'd never had a problem playing on his baby mat at the old place, but he seemed terrified to be left alone now. He'd screw his face up and cry, loud and strong, until someone picked him up again and held him close. As he grew out of that phase and learned to talk, he seemed to babble to an empty room as often as he spoke to his parents. And he would hold out cookies to an empty kitchen as if trying to share.

I don't remember who first voiced the word "ghost." I remember how hard John, so logical and grounded, fought to find rational explanations for the strange events. But with so many people around so often, at least three of us could say things like, "No, I watched you put the bottle in the sink: There's no other way it should be in the toy room now."

One night, eight of us were playing Team Capture the Flag on Xbox, and our friend Russ went to use the bathroom under the stairs. He came out and said, "All right, whoever needs the bathroom, I'm out: It's yours."

We all looked around at each other, baffled.

"No one needs the bathroom," our friend Sid said.

"The entire time I was in there, the handle was jiggling, like someone was trying to open the door," Russ said, wide eyed.

We counted out to him the four people in the living room and three more in the kitchen. No one in the house was close enough to the bathroom to turn the door handle.

The next Friday, my game controller went crazy. Instead of running down a hallway, my avatar stopped and started staring at the ceiling, spinning. I held up my controller with two fingers to show my teammates that I wasn't the one touching the joysticks. And every time we would finally be ready to go home, our shoes would be scattered up and down the stairs, instead of the neat rows we'd left them in when we took them off.

Things really escalated when John and Sabrina brought their new daughter home from the hospital eleven months after their son had been born. It seemed like the activity got kicked into high gear, as the invisible child tried to "help." The baby swing kept swinging after the batteries had died. The bassinet where the baby, Julie, was sleeping started shaking like it was in its own personal earthquake.

Every parent knows they'll wake up to the baby crying, asking for a middle-of-the-night feeding. But as often as not, Sabrina would wake up with Julie, give her a bottle and still hear a baby crying off in the distance. Even once Julie was sleeping through the night, the crying continued to wake the tired parents, who would find Julie sound asleep. Slowly, the crying would fade away.

Sabrina started begging John to move, and he kept trying to find explanations. Sabrina's part-time job was now house hunting. She hoped to find one perfect enough to convince John that they needed to get out.

That summer, Bristol City Historian Bud Phillips published *Pioneers in Paradise*. The book contained a full chapter of ghost stories from the city's early, early days. The one that caught my attention was called, "The High Ridge Children."

Phillips told the story as it was told to him. When the unnamed storyteller was young (she was 86 years old in 1953,) a family with three daughters had lived in an area called High Ridge when it was well outside the city limits. One bitterly cold winter, the two younger girls had died, possibly of pneumonia. They were buried by their very poor parents on the family's farm, and the oldest would often be found crying at their unmarked graves. Toward the end of spring, she died as well, and was buried beside them. The grief-stricken parents were never seen again, and it was assumed they'd left the area to start a new life. Afterwards, men hunting in the area would hear children crying, and search parties were often sent out to try and find what was assumed to be children lost and wandering in the ridges and valleys that now make up Steele Creek Park, the area just behind John and Sabrina's house. The searchers would never find the crying children, and Phillip's storyteller said it was just the "haint children."

About that same time, Bristol Parks and Rec published the first full map of the park's hiking trails. The ridge in the park that looked down on Broadway was called "East Ridge Loop." Now, in the days before online map services were available and easy to use, I could see for the first time how the trail on the ridge overlooked the small neighborhood. If the poor pioneer family lived in that area, they would be down in the valley, beside the creek, where the arable land was. The children the hunters heard crying, but could never find, might still be making their presence known in that little valley, where Boardwalk Avenue and my friends' house now sat.

Shortly after that, something finally happened that John couldn't explain away. Dozing in bed one morning, he woke up just enough to hear his son talking baby talk across the hall. Little Jonathan didn't seem to need anything; he was just talking to talk. Then, John heard a little girl's voice. Jonathan seemingly answered back, and the little girl answered again. At that point, John's conscious mind kicked into high gear. His wife was still asleep beside him. The baby was too young to speak. So who is talking to his son?

He sat upright in bed, wide awake. He could still hear Jonathan babbling, but now in the gaps in between where a conversation should have been happening, John could only hear silence. He woke Sabrina up and said, "We need to move."

The day before moving out, the kids were taken to their grandparents house so they wouldn't be in the way. That night, like so many nights before, Sabrina woke from a deep sleep to hear crying. This time, knowing neither of her children were in the house, she was immediately wide awake. But now, the house was filled with half-packed boxes, furniture disassembled in preparation to be loaded up. John's brother was sleeping in the children's room so he would be there bright and early to help fetch the moving truck.

This time, instead of fading, the crying coalesced into an audible, painful message. "Mommy, why are you leaving? Please don't go. Please don't leave us!"

That night there was no more sleep to be had for Sabrina. The next morning, she refused to let John and his brother leave her alone to get the truck until I arrived. They never spent another night in that house.

Almost a year later, as I passed by the neighborhood on my way somewhere else, I saw a couple of pink balloons tied to the mailbox that read "It's a Girl!" And I shivered despite the summer sun.

And one slow Saturday at the farmers market, nearly two decades later, I was telling a friend about these events. Her face brightened in recognition.

"I know exactly where that house is!" she said. "My son lives across the street. That poor little girl comes over all the time to play with my granddaughter's toys."

EMILY MONROE *was born in Bristol, Tennessee, a ninth generation Tennessean. She graduated from ETSU in 2006 with a English degree and a teaching license, and has since worked in educational jobs such as museums, nature centers, and as a substitute teacher. She also makes handmade soap to sell at farmers markets and craft shows, and is a member of the Holston Mountain Artisan's Guild. Her hobbies are traveling, writing, and gaming, especially Dungeons and Dragons with her two children.*

TWENTY-THREE
THE ODD CASE OF THE REVEREND DOCTOR STEPHEN FOSTER

KNOXVILLE, TENNESSEE

Kevin Saylor

There is a small graveyard in downtown Knoxville, situated on State Street just outside the doors of the First Presbyterian Church. It's an unassuming plot of land, just next door to a parking garage and only a block from the historic Tennessee Theatre. Hundreds of restaurant and theatre-goers pass by it every day, many of whom are unaware of its significance. Established sometime in the 1790s, it is the oldest graveyard in the city.

Among the two hundred twenty-some souls interred in the churchyard are prominent Knoxvillians such as Governor of the Southwest Territory William Blount and his wife Mary Grainger; U.S. Senator John Williams, who lost his Congressional seat to Andrew Jackson in 1823; Presbyterian minister Samuel Carrick, the founder of Blount College, which eventually became the University of Tennessee; and Knoxville founder James White.

Toward the back of the graveyard is a headstone belonging to the Reverend Stephen Foster. The stone is barely legible, the writing worn down by decades of wind, rain, and snow. It reads:

This stone is erected in Memory of the Rev. Stephen Foster Professor of Ancient Languages in East Tenn. College
The able Instructor of Youth
The faithful and devoted Minister of the Gospel
The Kind and affectionate Friend
He was born in Andover, Mass. Feb. 15, 1798 and amid the most eminent usefulness Respected, esteemed, beloved, Departed this life Jan. 11, 1835, aged 37 years
'Mysterious are Thy ways, O Lord!'

The learned Professor Foster was a bit more interesting than his tombstone might lead one to believe. Besides his duties teaching Greek and Latin at what is now the University of Tennessee, and for a time pastoring the Second Presbyterian Church, he was also Knoxville's version of a mad scientist.

Foster studied galvanism, a practice in which scientists conducted fairly crude experiments using electricity to stimulate biological tissue. The practice is named for Luigi Galvani, an Italian anatomy professor who in 1780 discovered he could animate the muscles of frog legs with electrical sparks.

Galvani's nephew, Giovanni Aldini, continued his uncle's experiments. In one particularly gruesome instance, he shocked the corpse of an ox until feces exploded out of its rectum. The experiments only got more morbid from there.

Eventually, galvanism's practitioners turned from animals to recently deceased humans. And that's where Knoxville's the Reverend Dr. Foster comes in.

A crowd of between 3,000-5,000 people gathered outside the city jail one summer afternoon in 1828, a large crowd even by today's standards. They were there for the spectator sport of the day: an execution.

The sheriff led two convicts outside at about one o'clock. The pair had committed a murder apiece.

The spectators sang a hymn while the two men climbed onto a horse drawn-cart. It took them to a place called Gallows Hill near what is today the northern end of Walnut Street downtown.

The first prisoner was Joshua Young, a man of about sixty-seven who tried to shoot his wife, failed, then finished the job with an axe. The second was James White (not the same James White who founded Knoxville). Sources differ on his age, but White was a handsome man of somewhere between twenty-four and forty who killed the husband of his lover and threw the body into a river.

The pair of convicts were noosed at the execution site. The ropes attached to two upright wooden posts about ten to twelve feet high connected by a beam. The men stood atop the wagon that brought them to the gallows.

While the men awaited their demise, a minister said a prayer and gave a sermon. The crowd sang another hymn. At about twenty minutes past two o'clock, the sheriff, a man named George White, yelled, "giddyap." The horses bolted and the two criminals dangled in the air until dead.

Someone cut down the bodies and the older man was buried in a shallow grave on the spot. But Stephen Foster had plans for the other corpse. The body of the young man was loaded onto a one-horse wagon and rushed down the hill to the Second Presbyterian Church. Much of the crowd followed.

Dr. Foster brought a sizable galvanic battery into the church. The lifeless body was carried into the modest brick building and the doors bolted shut. Some in the crowd scaled the wall of the church and looked through.

They observed as Dr. Foster fastened electrodes to the corpse, which were themselves connected to the battery. He flipped on the current. And then the corpse moved. And breathed again. Once. Twice. Three times. The crowd cheered. And Dr. Foster stopped the flow of electricity. Foster's interest was strictly philosophical. He had no interest in bringing back the dead. Or so he said.

After the experiment concluded, James White's family collected his remains and took them away, back to Marion County. But whether his body was still breathing when it left town is anyone's guess.

KEVIN SAYLOR *studied creative writing and journalism at the University of Tennessee. He spent fifteen years as a weekly freelance columnist for the* Knoxville News Sentinel, *covering local music, websites, entertainment, and writing the popular Notsville.com parody blog. His work has appeared in* East Tennessee Garden Stories; 23 Tales: Appalachian Ghost Stories, Legends & Other Mysteries; *and* 24 Tales: More Appalachian Ghost Stories, Legends & Other Mysteries. *He lives in Knoxville with his wife (who will not let him experiment on cadavers) and their three children.*

No. TWENTY-FOUR
MR. HARRISON'S HOUSE
RUSSELL COUNTY, VIRGINIA

Chrissie Anderson Peters

Jill Parsons loved Russell County, Virginia, and was thrilled to find a house there for her family. She and her two young sons, John and Tim, moved in around Christmas 2011. The brick ranch with an open basement had been built in 1969, the year Jill was born. The house had had one owner, Mr. Harrison, who died a year earlier and left the place empty, prompting his son to sell it. The basement had one finished room. Jill could tell the previous owner spent a good deal of time there because its fireplace had been well-used and its carpet worn. The rest of the house looked barely lived-in. It had lots of retro-seventies décor when she and her boys moved in.

They settled into the house during the holidays, excited to be in a new place and on their own. At times in her bedroom, though, Jill became uneasy. It felt like someone was sitting down at the bottom of her bed, a room neighbors said had been Mr. Harrison's at one point. Whenever she felt it, she found herself praying, or saying the Twenty-Third Psalm, which helped her calm down. But it didn't stop the feeling of someone coming to sit on the bottom of the bed. She wasn't afraid of Mr. Harrison's presence–she felt certain it was him. He wasn't threatening and wasn't malicious. And she had encountered other spirits in other places throughout her life. She was in tune with the spirit world, so it really didn't surprise her too much to find that she felt Mr. Harrison's presence in what had been his house.

One day, a few months after moving in, Jill went downstairs to wash clothes. She opened the door to the laundry room and gasped as she bumped into someone. She came face to face with the mirky image of an older man, a man she instantly knew must be Mr. Harrison. He was visible from the waist up, more faint the farther down she looked. And his expression showed he was as surprised as she was, surprised that *she* could see *him*, she thought at the time. She could see through the apparition but saw it solidly enough to know it was a man, solidly enough to see that look of amazement on his face before he faded in front of her, as she held her breath in anticipation of what might happen next. It would be the only time she saw Mr. Harrison, but not the first or last time he made his presence known.

She spoke nothing of the ghostly encounter with John and Tim, who were ten and eight at the time. Mr. Harrison continued sitting on Jill's bed, and she began hearing noises in the house after seeing him. She knew some people would have said the noises were just "house" noises, but after seeing Mr. Harrison and feeling him sit on her bed numerous times, Jill was convinced not everything she heard was just an old house settling. She felt certain at least some of it was an old man's spirit wandering about his former home.

In 2015, Jill married Tom Adams. Tom loved music, and after a couple of years, he built a music room in the basement. When he and his friends got together to jam, Jill frequently noticed that two electrical cords that hung in loops beside each other would move rhythmically in time to the music. Initially, she thought it might be vibrations from the equipment, or maybe the air was moving them. But she quickly realized they sometimes moved in one direction together, then they would change and sway in opposite directions. Something-or someone-was keeping time with the music during those jam sessions. It made her smile to think of Mr. Harrison enjoying Tom's band.

These little things went on for years, with Jill not giving much thought to them. She knew Mr. Harrison was still in the house, but he wasn't hurting anything, really. He didn't knock over things. He didn't hide things. He wasn't aggressive. He just liked sitting on beds and keeping time with music, so far as she could tell. What was the harm in that?

When John was about sixteen, though, Mr. Harrison changed. One day, John and his friend Alex were sitting in the room downstairs, hanging out. They were the only ones home-or so they thought. John heard something briefly at the bottom of the steps, then heard it suddenly run up the steps-audibly pounding every step loudly-and slammed the door open when it reached the top of the stairs. The door had been closed, as was the practice of everyone when they went from the upstairs to the basement or the basement to the upstairs. The boys rushed over to the steps and looked up in confusion. The door was wide open. They called out. No one answered. They had heard someone running up the stairs, but no one was there, no one was visible to them at all. Yet they both heard it.

The boys looked at each other.

"What the hell just happened?" John exclaimed.

Then the two boys ran up the steps themselves, leaving the basement door untouched, and fled the house in John's car.

The steps became a source of trouble. After the day John and Alex experienced someone running up the stairs, the door was not only shut, but it was locked at all times when someone wasn't using the steps to go downstairs to get something. It became common for Jill and John to hear Mr. Harrison walking up the steps, heavy-footed, and turning the doorknob once he reached the top, shaking it. They could hear his hand on the rails as he went up and down the steps, too. It was terrifying, especially for John.

Tim never heard it, or if he did, he never said anything to anyone about it.

Mr. Harrison traversed the stairs often when John was home alone, and Jill received many phone calls from her frightened older son while she was out getting dinner or buying groceries, asking her to please hurry and come home because "he" was at it again.

That was around 2017. Jill had patiently shared her home with Mr. Harrison for six years. She had been fine with him sitting on beds and playing with cords, even with him making a little noise around the house occasionally. But now he was messing with her children.

It had to stop.

She went to the laundry room in the basement–because she often felt his presence there–and laid down the rules. It wasn't just his house now, and it was time he realized it and acted accordingly.

"I don't mind if you live here," Jill told him, "but you will not scare my children!" She paused, then added a little more softly, "We're trying to love your home and take care of it. I want to raise my family here, just like you did yours. Let me do that."

That was about eight years ago. Mr. Harrison still sometimes listens in when Tom and his buddies play music, moving the electrical cords back and forth. Sometimes Jill still senses his presence in other ways, although he doesn't sit down on her bed now. He quit stomping up the stairs and turning the doorknob. He quit scaring John and his friends. It was as though he had to be reminded: it wasn't his house, anymore, really–it belonged to a new family, and he needed to behave better if he was going to stay there. So, he has.

A native of Southwest Virginia, **CHRISSIE ANDERSON PETERS** *now lives in Bristol, Tennessee. Peters holds degrees from Emory & Henry College and the University of Tennessee. Her writing has appeared in* Still: The Journal, Pine Mountain Sand & Gravel, Clinch Mountain Review, Mildred Haun Review, Women of Appalachia Project, Salvation South, Cutleaf, 23 Tales: Appalachian Ghost Stories, Legends & Other Mysteries, *and* 24 Tales: More Appalachian Ghost Stories, Legends & Mysteries. *Her books include* Dog Days and Dragonflies, Running From Crazy, *and* Blue Ridge Christmas. *She loves travel and anything from the eighties.*

TWENTY-FIVE
SHADOWS HAVE NO EYES

CHARLOTTESVILLE, VIRGINIA

Jay Herrin

I met Rust five years ago on the night of the Summer Solstice. I was invited to a country estate and arrived to find a clearing in the woods where thirty feet of roaring flame cloaked the sky. A posse of drummers rattled and thumped in the shadow of the vast bonfire, their faces cast in deep, ochre contours. They stoked a crowd with voices hoarse from screaming. Many wore animal skins, or sported antler crowns, or masked their faces in frightening bones.

Rust stood out for his lack of effort. Jeans and a *Metallica* shirt. Dark, greasy bangs. He was smoking a Marlboro, and he hadn't shaved. He was with his sister, Elise, who I knew from parties in town. She was all smiles and clearly drunk. He was neither.

I asked if he was enjoying himself. He shrugged.

The evening rocked and bent. We swayed to chanting. I shouted nonsense at the spark-choked sky. Eventually, we rested on some stumps under the pine boughs at the edge of the clearing, where I suggested we share ghost stories. Another friend of mine told the tale of a spirit that haunted his grandmother's farm. There were shudders. Laughter.

Rust lit another cigarette and leaned toward us on his elbows. "I've a story," he said. "If y'all wanna hear it."

Rust's drawl was thick, and his memory stalled. Elise, uneasy, didn't help him. I gathered they'd been raised at the tip of Southwest Virginia, at the mountains' threshold. A quiet place where wind chimes sounded more than car horns, Rust finally said, and antique souvenir shops gathered dust.

Their mom drove them thirty minutes each morning to Oakwood, the nearest town with an elementary school, Twin Valley. There, Rust met Stella. Stella wore long-sleeved turtleneck shirts, even in summer when they'd make her red and sweaty. She gave out unwanted hugs. She had nervous ticks, like if someone tried to take her picture she'd start crying. She was known as the kid who once soiled herself in class.

Rust said he hadn't cared about those things. He liked the frightening drawings she made in art class of people screaming and spitting fire. They'd become friends, making pretend oddity shops at recess. Fondness seeped into his face as he talked. Frown lines slackened.

On Wednesdays, when Elise would stay after school for one of her clubs, Rust would ride in Stella's rickety truck with her strong-armed dad to their cabin, a nook buried in the oaks halfway up what was left of the mountain after the mining company sheared off the top and ripped out its veins. They'd taken the jobs with them when they left, but not the cabin.

Rust especially stumbled when describing Stella's home. He mentioned some hunting trophies, a shed with worker's tools, dusty walls. The windows had spiderwebbed panes, he noted, then quickly said Stella's dad was friendly to him.

"But Stella was right nasty to him," he muttered, the cigarette brushing his untrimmed chin. "Talkin' back. Snarling. Always avoiding him. Guess we were all sorta rude to our old folks, but I'd think with just the one you'd feel what you had."

Rust and Stella mostly played outside until his mom picked

him up after dinner, finding fairy rings or collecting dried leaves to make witch potions. Stella would call the potions 'protection spells.' Said they made the drinker untouchable. Once she even tried to drink one. She'd gotten sick.

At this point in his story Rust's eyes darkened as though he forgot we were there. A tremor joined his voice as he recounted, more to the forest hollow than us, that he'd gone home with Stella one Wednesday. He recalled the cabin feeling stiff that day. Stella's dad served them burnt carrots. Her eyes stayed on the floor while she ate. Pieces of a broken lamp were strewn across the couch, and no one had picked them up.

When they'd eaten, Stella declared the two of them were going all the way up the mountain. Up to where the abandoned tracks of the mining trucks formed a giant maze of nothing.

Twilight loomed over their hike. Cicadas hummed. Creatures scurried out of sight in the canopy. Lichen watched from the skin of boulders. Rust told us how he'd planted his foot on an old log, and it sunk straight through the rotten wood into a nest of writhing termites. That had been the sign to turn back. Later, a branch snagged Stella's turtleneck at her throat and pulled it down, and he noticed her neck had purple marks. Like the shirt was throttling her.

Finally, they'd crested a clump of onion grass to where the mountain had been beheaded. A plateau of dirt. Lifeless. Before he could ask to turn around, Stella scrambled away over the dirt and gravel. Rust grew breathless keeping up with her. He finally caught her at the bottom of a small dirt gulley, framed by a dark awning standing out from the wasteland. A huge heap of wet soil and gravel muddled the ground around it, and a shovel stood to one side.

Stella told him the rain had found the cave. She just finished the job.

Rust glowered at the cave entrance. He told us with an ashen face how he'd been wary of the crack in the rock. All the local kids knew unmarked caves were dangerous, and the two of them had no flashlight or lantern. But as dusk settled over the mountain's barren scalp, Stella casually stepped into the blackness. Rust, panicked, followed.

The dark was sudden. Rust's footsteps echoed in the rocky crevice. He'd reached out a tentative hand to brush the walls. They were damp and jagged. The light from the entrance cast his shadow before him, long and wiry, and barely illuminated Stella's back. She strode forward, tall and proud. Above, the crevice quickly opened up, the ceiling drifting away into an impenetrable gloom.

He asked her, quietly, if she'd been in the cave before. She shushed him.

Rust was cautious only to move his feet where Stella had already stepped, which meant when she stopped, he nearly crashed into her.

He asked what was wrong. She didn't move. Rust wasn't the clingy type, but he gripped her shoulder tightly as he peered past it to see for himself.

Rust paused his story here. One bonfire chant ended and the drums struck a new beat. Elise was frowning.

"There was some *thing* in that dark," he said, leaning forward on the stump with his knees pressed together. "Somethin'... *standing*. Tall. Taller'n any person I've seen. Just half an outline. Might've been a trick of the light, a strange shape in the rock, 'cept that it... I could hear breathing. Ragged breathing. Low, shudderin' breaths, an' they rasped like mountain wind. Couldn't have come from one of us. Never heard a person make such a sound."

He hadn't moved. He was terrified that if the light shifted at all the possibility that he was just seeing things would vanish. But Stella, he told us in whisper, she'd taken a step forward. And when she had, the figure—the faceless, looming, spindly thing in the dark—had taken a step back.

Stella again pressed forward.

The figure mirrored her.

Rust stumbled forward as well, his legs moving against his will. They were most afraid of being separated from Stella. But when he moved, he could have sworn twin pits of silver light sparked to life in the onyx black. They hovered above. He thought of piercing eyes. Rust grabbed Stella's shirt from the back, yanking. Begging her to turn. To leave. To *run*. But Stella didn't move. Instead, she stood on her tiptoes, reached up towards the silver eyes... and laid her hand on solid rock, the back of the cave.

Rust's eyes adjusted to the light then, and he saw that the spot where the silver eyes had been was actually from where a quartz vein ran through the rock. A pair of protruding crystals caught some fragment of sun from the distant cave entrance. The breathing seemed to fade to the whistle of wind.

"I thought I was losin' it," he said. "Them eyes, they'd been so bright. And the breaths... "

Stella, unfazed, bent to pick something off the cave floor. She showed Rust what it was: a bowie knife with a hand-carved handle. The kind used to skin deer. Whether their eyes had been playing tricks or not, someone had been in the cave before. They'd left their knife on the ground. And if the cave hadn't been open until recently, that meant they couldn't have gone far.

"*Let's go*," Rust begged, and Stella finally agreed. But she'd taken the knife with her.

At home that night, Rust lay awake in bed. The shape and the sound of the breathing stuck to him. He'd tried telling Elise about it. A decade later in our story circle she grumbled and accused him of an overactive imagination. He simply recited her old reply.

"Ya know, Russel," she'd giggled at him, "*some a' the girls in my class say when they cut the mountains, things came out. Old things. Things that should'a stayed locked up in that dark.*" Then she'd laughed again and told him to go to sleep.

He had not.

Rust was reluctant to go back to Stella's house after that. He told his mom he'd rather wait at Elise's clubs. He still saw Stella at school, and they'd draw their gory pictures like always. But soon after he stopped going over, Stella started to change. She stopped wearing long turtlenecks. She put her hair up in a ponytail, and she didn't give people sudden hugs anymore.

Rust hadn't given it much thought. Lots of kids changed as they got older. But one evening, his mom was busy late. Too late for him to stay with Elise, who had gone home with her friend, and Rust... he was forced to return to the cabin.

So he'd sat in the backseat of Stella's truck. Same old truck as always, he said. The engine grumbling up a storm. But Rust was uneasy. For one, Stella had greeted her dad with a smile. She'd never smiled at him like that as long as Rust had known her. Her dad turned the wheel more stiff than usual, like he'd been injured. Rust noticed a line of stitches healing across his forehead, like he'd suffered a fall. And Rust hadn't liked the sputtering groan of the truck engine anymore. It reminded him of the breathing they'd heard in the dark.

The cabin was different, too. Cleaner. The broken lamp had been cleaned up. Stella's dad cooked them carrot slices, and they were delicious. Salted. Tender. Stella even thanked him. Rust felt prickly. He asked to play outside.

He followed Stella to the old tool shed. She told him to wait outside as she unlocked it, but he glanced past her. Saws, shears, and hoes hung from rusted hooks. A table lurked in one corner, stained a dark color. A knife lay amidst a flurry of score marks. Rust only glimpsed it for an instant, but he swore it was the bowie knife they found in the cave.

Then Stella reappeared dragging a cornhole set. She glared at him and shut the door quickly. Rust had thought they'd make potions, like always, but Stella said they were too old for potions. She wanted to toss the beanbags.

They idly threw the beanbags back and forth as the sun went down. Rust noticed that Stella had brought the shovel back down the mountain. It rested against the shed, planted in the dirt. The surrounding soil was red and wet. Like it'd been overturned. Stella followed his eyes and nodded. She was starting a garden, she told him. She'd grow her own carrots.

Finally, as the dark settled in, Rust's mom came to get him. He made a quick goodbye and climbed into the backseat. Stella and her dad stood in the rearview mirror, waving and smiling.

The last rays of sun struck the mirror, and the reflection changed. For a blink, two specks of silver light gleamed in the glass, burning like eyes straight into Rust's own. Rust panicked. A deep, unending terror filled his heart. His soul, he knew, was drowning. But he was unable to look away. Unable to even blink as the eyes of pure silver bored into him.

And then they *were* eyes: Stella's dad's eyes, their usual chestnut brown, and he was smiling in the reflection at Rust. And then, their truck trundled around the bend.

When Rust finished talking, we all sat in silence for a minute. Elise was the first to move. She made an excuse and quickly left. The rest of us were rigid. I thought of the faceless thing in the dark. Of the knife. The scourings in the wood. The stitch marks.

"You don't think…?" I murmured, finding my throat dry. Then I shook myself. Elise had said it. Rust has an overactive imagination. Many of us liked to make stories out of circumstance.

But Rust never answered me. He got up and said he needed to find his sister, and I haven't seen him since.

JAY HERRIN *is a fourth grade teacher in Charlottesville, Virginia. They've spent most of their life in Virginia, including graduating from The College of William & Mary in 2017 and getting their master's degree in teaching from the University of Virginia in 2022. When not teaching, Jay loves to read, garden, tinker with various writing projects, and go hiking in the Blue Ridge Mountains and Shenandoah National Park.*

Send us your ghost stories

We hope you enjoyed *25 Tales: Even More Appalachian Ghost Stories & Mysteries*.

Check out our previous anthologies at howlinghillspublishing.com. And if you have a true story set in Greater Appalachia that you'd like to share, please email it to submissions@howlinghillspublishing.com. They can include personal experiences, family stories, or reporting on other quirky events or mysteries.

Submission guidelines:
- Stories must be set in Greater Appalachia.
- We won't consider fiction or poetry.
- Length should be between 500 to 5,000 words.
- Payment for accepted stories depends on length and includes two contributor copies.
- While submissions for our anthologies are always open, the deadline for *26 Tales* is March 15, 2026
- We'll provide feedback if submissions arrive early enough.

–**Terry Shaw**
Howling Hills Publishing

www.ingramcontent.com/pod-product-compliance
Lightning Source LLC
Chambersburg PA
CBHW070633030426
42337CB00020B/3998